# Invitations Everywhere

## SAY YES, AS DEE GRUENIG DID

*C. Warren Gruenig*

Mary + Fred - what SPECIAL
people. Dee + I are
lucky to have you as
friends.

8/22/17

C. W. [signature]

W0006119

www. InvitationsEverywhere . com

**Invitations Everywhere: Say Yes as Dee Gruenig Did**

© 2015 C. Warren Gruenig

Library of Congress Cataloging-in-Publication Data

C. Warren Gruenig

Life's Invitations are Everywhere: Dee Gruenig's experiences with accepting them

1. Self-help. 2. Spiritual. 3. Personal Growth.

**Library of Congress Control Number: 2015912305**

CreateSpace Independent Publishing Platform,
North Charleston, SC

**ISBN-13: 978-1515215790**

**ISBN-10: 1515215792**

Cover Design: Fiona Jayde, FionaJaydeMedia.com
Interior Design: Tamara Cribley, DeliberatePage.com
Website Design: Wendi Liechty, LagunaBeachMedia.com
Editing: Mary Harris, MaryHarrisWriter.com

# Praise for *Invitations Everywhere*

"The Junior League of Orange County is thrilled to hear about the publication of Dee Gruenig's story. League members fondly remember her participation in the organization's The Christmas Company® event. Member Mary Earl Spencer says 'Yes, it began with The Christmas Company in 1983. Our Exhibitor Chairs told me about this great gal who was doing home parties selling rubber stamps. I remember thinking, Rubber stamps? Really?!! They signed her up to be an exhibitor. She was our top seller— by far!! She was so enthusiastic, such a lovely person and a joy to have as an exhibitor.' And that was the beginning of a great relationship between Dee, Posh Presents, the Junior League, and The Christmas Company®."

**Dr. Carla Dillon,** President, Junior League
of Orange County, California, Inc.

"Dee Gruenig's openness to new challenges and her unwavering faith in all that is good, have resulted in a life lived to the fullest. Dee's personal and professional experiences reveal the joy and personal fulfillment that came from that faith and innocence— old-fashioned concepts that are eternal and universal. It has been a privilege to know and work with both Dee and Warren. This poignant book will always remind me of them and the joie de vivre that is the core of their relationship and their world view."

**Mike McCooey,** President/CEO, Plaid Enterprises, Inc.; Past
President of Association of Crafts & Creative Industries (ACCI) and
The Craft & Hobby Association (CHA)

"Mere words do not describe Dee Gruenig and the gifts she brought to the craft industry. Her audacious energy, infectious joy, and outrageous creativity helped fuel the movement that brought so many blessings to so many people. It was my pleasure to work with Dee in teaching the creative ways our products— rubber stamps and stickers—could illustrate the values and emotions that people want to share. Dee will be honored for her indomitable spirit but her real gift to us is her heart. May God continue to bless this precious woman."

**Andrea Grossman,** President, Mrs. Grossman's Paper Company

"In our first ever All Star special issue, we featured eighteen outstanding artists and leaders who have been dynamic in our industry, building it and sustaining it. We featured Dee Gruenig right up front. She has been a superstar from the first with rubber stamping and scrapbooking, being successful in all aspects she entered of the craft industry. She was an artist, founder, and president of her own company, retailer, board member of two separate industries, television personality, and writer. She was regularly booked as a featured speaker at conventions and public venues on five continents. A loving, can-do attitude made her stand out."

**Kelly Herrold,** Editor, *Scrap & Stamp Arts Magazine*

"I thought that I knew Dee. She was on my TV show for 72 segments and we've been friends forever, but I just discovered that I knew only a smidgen about her 'other' life and the places she's been, and the people she's met, and the folks that she's taught. This book is a tell-all kick! Good thing her husband spilled the beans or we might never have known."

**Carol Duvall,** ABC Television's *Home Show* 1988-1994; HGTV's *Carol Duvall Show* 1994-2005

"Over my 43-year career in interior design, I taught for a period Basics of Residential Design. I had one student who stood out… Dee Gruenig. Sitting in class, her face shone with light and her mind absorbed the essence of all I wanted to import. It is no surprise that Dee went on to achieve so much success in an artistic field."

**Lee Mink,** ASID. Designer of corporate interiors for Occidental Petroleum, Unocal, and select residential projects.

"Dee Gruenig is an inspiration to many of us in the rubber stamp community. She's done just about everything a rubber stamp company owner can do — and she's done it well. I was honored to be invited on one of Dee's crafting cruises and saw first-hand her dedication to stamp art and her incredible work ethic. I've always admired the Posh Impressions stamp line and the skill with which Dee demonstrated techniques at shows, in classes, on television and videos. I've always admired Dee's people skills. She's a shining example of how to treat colleagues, customers, and staff — always with respect and love. It's my pleasure to count Dee and her husband Warren as special friends."

**Roberta Sperling,** Founder and Editor,
*RubberStampMadness Magazine*

"Dee is known for color, so with us it was a perfect marriage. She discovered our pens, markers and ink pads for stamping back in 1979 and this transformed rubber stamping to a world of color. Her energy and love for everything she did impacted our company in a dynamic way. She was immensely popular and successful because of her amazing creativity and for the wonderful way she worked with everyone."

**Go Iida,** Chief Operating Office, Uchida of America

"Stamping as a form of crafting was completely unknown in South Africa when I started my business in 1987. I traveled to the HIA Craft Fair in the United States and was stunned when I watched Dee using stamps in the most creative ways that I'd never thought possible. I planned a local craft fair for my South Africa the following year, and I knew that the one person I had to invite as a guest would be Dee. She took stamping to a whole new level, and was the star of the show!"

**Joan Launspach**, Former Owner, Stamps Unlimited, Krugersdorp, South Africa

"Dee Gruenig was the pioneer for rubber stamping. It became so popular with her books, videos, and public appearances that the LA Mart in Los Angeles created an event called *Rubber Stamp Mania*. It was immensely successful, doubling in size each year of its existence. It couldn't have been successful without Dee and I owe her everything. She was the "stud," meaning principal support, of the rubber stamping craze."

**John Weiglein,** President, LA Mart, 1991-2000

"In 1994-2000, I sent Dee to teach art instructors at Army installations in Germany, Korea, Hawaii, and several installations in the Continental United States. In my thirty-two year career with Army Arts and Crafts, Dee was the most exuberant, hardworking, and talented art instructor I had the pleasure of working with."

**Janice A. Osthus,** Program Manager, United States Army Arts and Crafts

"Dee is known for her bold personality and images! During Stampin' Up!'s early years, Dee was a favorite at our annual conventions, masterfully making her images come alive with vibrant color!"

**Shelli Gardner,** President, Stampin' Up

"Our company looked to trendsetting creatives like Dee. We had the honor of translating her images, color ways, and ideas into paper products the likes of which no one has created since. Thoughtful, passionate, and overflowing with excitement and creativity — that's Dee, a true one-of-a-kind creation!"

**David Wilke,** Past President, Paper Adventures

"I once published an editorial tribute to Dee Gruenig. I was impressed because of her graciousness and sincerity when I met her at a convention. At that time, I had a temporary disfigurement on my face that seemed to make people extremely uncomfortable when speaking with me, but not Dee. She was comfortable in my presence and genuinely kind. Her natural demeanor also quickly put me at ease. Her reputation was that she treated everyone that way, and that it was one of the reasons her business flourished. People wanted to work with her."

**Cyndi Duncan,** Founder and Editor, *Altered Arts Magazine*

Dee Gruenig was one of the pioneers in the craft industry, especially in rubber stamps, and her influence continues to be felt today. She has a smile that lights up a room. I was first inspired by Dee's talent at product development when I coordinated a line of her rubber-stamp images for Marian Heath (one of my greeting card industry clients). She was a pleasure to work with, a consummate professional whose warmth and charm are exceeded only by her big heart and innate talent. Most impressive, Dee's fabulous videos helped set the standard for teaching online, and taking a workshop with Dee is something people always remember. I consider her a visionary, and feel blessed to count her among my friends!

**Joanne Fink,** Founder, Zenspirations®;
President, Lakeside Designs

"We met Dee at a rubber stamp store in the 1990s. She was already an icon in the industry. Taken with her approachable and infectious personality, we knew Dee would be a great fit with Ranger products. It wasn't long before the Rainbow Sponge was born! We shared fun times with Dee and Warren, both personally and professionally. Thanks for the memories!"

**Anne and Vince DiLascia,** Former Owners, Ranger Industries, Inc.

"I first met Dee when she and her husband attended one of our annual All Night Media Stamp Camps sometime in the late 1970s. I doubt either of us had the faintest idea of the way in which stamps would take over our lives for the next few decades. Dee's warmth, intelligence, enthusiasm, and creativity made her a shining star and contributed to the success she achieved and so rightfully deserved."

**Marilyn Freund,** Founder and President, All Night Media, Inc., 1975-1999

"Bright, sunny, sparking, and passionate are just a few words that describe Dee. We rarely see her without a huge smile and a twinkle in her eye. But really, these words only define the surface of an incredibly fun creative, energetic, and generous person. Always there to share stories, experiences, techniques, and ideas — her enthusiasm is contagious. She's motivated countless people with the confidence that they too are artistic and creative. Never a derogatory comment, always supportive, constructive and nurturing…Dee has done a ton for our industry. She is the best teacher, coach, and friend. We can't thank her enough for opening her arms to us!"

**Judi Watanabe,** Owner, JudiKins, Inc.

# DEDICATION

*To my amazing wife who daily
demonstrates the contents of this book.*

# Table of Contents

# Foreword

With a title like *Invitations Everywhere,* how could I refuse C.W. Gruenig's invitation to write this forward? While the book chronicles his wife's success in the rubber stamping business, it gives testament to the unseen hands that continually guided her on her journey of success. Instead of fighting to accomplish great things, which often seems to be the norm for businesses, Dee welcomed each opportunity as an invitation from God to share her passion for creativity.

She was fortunate to have a partner like C.W. While many men would have had a difficult time supporting their mate, C.W. became Dee's devoted cheerleader and later, an integral part of her business.

Having known C.W. for the past five years, I have witnessed his genuine love for Dee and his passionate desire to share her story with the world. In the process, he created a book that offers readers a wonderful gift to see invitations everywhere.

According to C.W. and Dee, we receive invitations every day. They come in many different forms. Often we don't know that we've been given them. We may be invited to recognize and seize opportunities, establish relationships with strangers, exercise creativity, and deepen our faith.

Once we get an invitation, we can accept or decline. Saying yes to invitations opens doors of possibilities. Saying no keeps them closed. Spirit-driven invitations open doors to personal and spiritual growth. Once we say yes, all we need do is show up and be touched by the experience.

This book caused me to reflect on my own life. All too often,

I drove myself to climb the mountain of success. While this did help me accomplish many goals, I realized that I could have relaxed more on the journey so that Spirit could gently guide me on the way.

*Invitations Everywhere* has inspired me to become more like Dee, who said yes to sharing her passion with the world. Doing so opened doors of success and enriched her and her husband's lives.

Thank you, C.W. Gruenig, for sharing Dee's life with us and offering us a precious invitation to connect with our Inner Guidance. You remind us to see invitations everywhere as opportunities to share our talents and gifts with the world. If we remember that we are not alone, but guided by unseen hands, we open our lives to countless blessings and amazing miracles.

**Leonard Szymczak,** Author of *The Roadmap Home:*
*Your GPS to Inner Peace*

# Introduction

Dee and I have known each other for almost twenty years, and we worked together on television for ten of those years. We are friends. I figured I knew her well. What I didn't realize was that there was a lot that I didn't know about her life beyond television and rubber stamping.

The majority of the time we have spent together has been inside a television studio where we spent as much time laughing as we did talking, so perhaps my version of "life with Dee" might be quite a bit different from what you will read on the coming pages. It was that realization that gave me an idea about writing this introduction. It would be not as much about what Dee has done, but who she is.

I decided to ask some of our mutual friends and co-workers how they would describe Dee, and requested that they give me single word answers. They did. A lot of single words.

"Enthusiastic," "Enthusiastic," "Enthusiastic,"…that's not a computer error, folks. Those were the words given on the first three responses I received. This was all done by e-mail so no collaboration was involved. Then came two more "enthusiastic" responses, but they could not manage to limit themselves to only one word. These read "infectiously enthusiastic." There were others, of course, including "vivacious" and "effervescent" and "Hi-Octane." Even "supercalifragilisticexpialidocious" made the list.

No wonder Dee was such a popular guest on our show. It wasn't just the viewers who found her enthusiasm contagious. She was fun to work with. She was always so prepared, yet ready to go with whatever might happen. She was a joy, and that was another word on the list.

Without ever meeting Dee, I think that from that list you would get a pretty good picture of the kind of person she is.

But wait, there's more!

Dee's talents go on and beyond rubber stamping and television, which she demonstrated at the opening night cocktail party on a Carol Duvall Crafting Cruise. We had hoped to find some suitable talent to entertain the crafters. Little did we guess that it would be Dee who would be the evening's showstopper.

All teachers had been challenged to wear an outfit that cost less than $20. There were a number of Michaels Crafts Stores' boas in evidence, and jeweled ensembles, even a plastic table runner with floor length fringe worn as a party dress. Then Dee walked in. She had found a discount store and was stunning in a strapless fuchsia full-length gown. $20.00? Yes, the $19.95 price tag hanging on a string pinned to her bodice à la Minnie Pearl proved it.

But when it was time for live performances, she really stole the show with her Spoonerism rendition of "Cinderella and The Handsome Prince." In Spoonerism, the title became "Prinderella and the Prandsome Hinse." It's a story that will give you poosegimples and make your cresh fleep.

She recited the entire fairy tale with a proper and appropriate dramatic rendering. Everybody loved it. She would have received a standing ovation if we hadn't already been standing.

Now read on and learn even more about this delightful woman and the places she's been and the life that she's led.

**Carol Duvall**
ABC Television's *Home Show,* 1988-1994
HGTV's *Carol Duvall Show,* 1994-2005

# Preface

*Our deepest wishes are whispers of our authentic selves. We must learn to respect them. We must learn to listen.*

Sarah Ban Breathnach

This book has been written because my wife's career was amazingly unusual, and hopefully, it will be beneficial to inspire you the reader. For thirty years, she was given enticing invitations. She accepted them. It is my hope that my writing what actually happened will benefit you and others.

The invitations came unexpectedly from individuals, organizations, manufacturers, and media. Rarely was she familiar with any of those extending them. Nearly all of them came as surprises. Some involved learning and challenges, but that made them special, to make Dee grow.

Right up front I will say that this book provides no formulas, no magic bullets, and no list of precisely what to do. It tries to say how Dee thought about her day, her life, and the world around her.

She believed that invitations and opportunities are everywhere, and they come from a God who loves everyone. We need to pay attention. Call God the Source, the Universe, Creator, Love, the Christ Presence, Allah, Divine Mind. Use any term that you like. Use what fits for *you*. Preferably, make your premise a God of Love rather than a punishing God. Choose thinking that encourages, energizes, and inspires you. All of us can choose what we believe, what we think, and how we choose to feel, so choose beliefs that will serve you. Why choose anything else? Dee believed that the Universe wants what is good for her. She believed it with all her heart.

Before Dee began her thirty-year career, which I will discuss in this book, we were both public school educators. She was a teacher, and I taught before becoming an elementary school principal. As a side job, to increase income, we sold a program for life planning, and we put the long range planning program to use for ourselves. Our plans produced as many disappointments as successes, and it was stressful and sometimes disappointing as we doggedly kept to our plans with mixed results. Long-range planning with firm goals, objectives, tasks, and time lines work for many; I am not discounting them if they work for you. But if they produce disappointments, stress, and blinders to what else is available, you might want to try something different. Long-range planning can work in conjunction with prayerful inspiration. Just be flexible and ready to change direction when you get a better idea, and say yes to invitations and opportunities.

How do you know if invitations received are beneficial? Research them, of course, and listen in contemplation. There should be a good feeling about them, a feeling of peace and a feeling that they are honest and fair. If not, beware. It gets down to faith and trust that prayerful listening, with whatever religious or nonreligious background you have, is a steadfast guide.

After seventeen years in the classroom, Dee left teaching and "planned" differently than the steadfast planning for the future that we were both taught. Every morning she prayed, meaning she listened expectedly for inspiration, support, and inner guidance. She believed that all good things were available. She listened for what to do and expected an answer. She put joy and energy into her day as the first thing to do. She put God first, and she chose to toss out fear and negative thinking. She was, and is today, outstanding with short-term planning, usually in written form, once she gets a message for what is best to do. Though trained in long-range planning, she didn't use it because she learned that when she remained open to inspiration, inner guidance led to invitations. I would tease her with the question, "What do you want to be doing in five years?" She didn't know and didn't want to know.

I continued to write firm plans for the future in a variety of areas and measure my results. Results were a mixture of good and bad. Many goals and objectives simply didn't materialize. This was not true with Dee. She was having doors open wide for her. There were many of them, and invitations were consistent. Her way was working better than mine.

I listened prayerfully each morning, as Dee did, but holding to *my* plans; I was focused straight ahead, with little deviation. If ideas or "invitations" were coming my way, I seldom paid attention. If I paid attention, and was aware of them, I didn't trust them. I held to my personal goals and objectives. I was looking for results with what *I* wanted, instead of what was best all the way around.

I felt that things would be fine *when* plans I initially had for Dee's business were realized. Dee was grateful *before* seeing anything happen, and she didn't choose what the results had to be. She didn't keep a list. She believed that whatever happened would be good. Moreover, she *felt* that all would be good and it was. Wayne Dyer said we will see it when we believe it. With Dee, "it" was not a specific thing, but rather an adventurous, trustful conviction that something good was on its way.

I have learned to trust in Dee's way. It is so much easier and I don't miss the *Aha* ideas, the opportunities that are everywhere when I am open to them. The opportunities should be blessings and they should make the recipient a better person.

Especially important is to take action. Many people get good ideas, even specific invitations, and take no action. This might be due to doubt, fear, distraction, lack of trust in the Creator, or lack of trust in ourselves. Inspiration Dee received produced enthusiasm. She called her enthusiasm "passion." She wanted to share her passion that was creativity expressed through art because she believed it would benefit others. She wanted to title the book, *I Share With Passion,* but I chose *Invitations Everywhere* because every opportunity *was* an invitation. They were invitations we couldn't plan or take credit for. Additionally, the title she wanted could be twisted with adolescent comments placed on YouTube and Twitter, which sadly we have seen happen.

Reiterating, Dee gave up long-term planning and few had better short-term planning and organizational skills than Dee. She was known for them. HGTV televised a short presentation about her organization, filmed in her home studio. You can see it and another video at www.InvitationsEverywhere.com

She had her head on straight so that she could be successful with the invitations received. The thirty years of consistent experiences described in this book showed me the importance of being open to invitations and opportunities that are abundantly everywhere, when through prayerful inspiration and trust, we are willing to be receptive to them.

Should you be listening for directions to the good that is waiting for you? I think you might know what to do in your own way.

**C. Warren Gruenig**
Happy Husband

# Chapter One

## Two Invitations — How I Met Dee

*Be open to invitations, even something you may not want to accept. Consider carefully. They can open doors to wonderful opportunities.*

— Anonymous

In the summer of 1966, I was invited by a distant friend to a swim party that I did not really want to attend. I expected it to be boring. Besides, my dad had taken me to a golf tournament to watch the legendary Ben Hogan play one of his last matches, and I was enjoying the day with Dad. I learned later from my wife-to-be that she had received the same invitation and, like me, didn't want to attend. However, we both accepted and it was the best invitation acceptance of my life.

At the party, held in a fenced backyard with a swimming pool large for a private home, I was taken with a cute blonde on the other side of the yard. Whenever I caught glimpses of her, I noticed she snuck glances at me as well. Throughout the evening, we never got close enough to speak. Then, as she and her younger sister walked past me to leave just before 9:00 p.m., I grasped Dede Davenport, later to be called Dee Gruenig, by the hand and introduced myself to her and her sister Bonnie. Almost immediately we three became aware that our favorite television program, *Get Smart*, with Don Adams, was about to begin. We darted into the living room to watch. Afterward, Dede and I strolled to the pool just a few yards away.

Everyone had swimsuits under their street clothes. Dede was first to strip to hers and she silently slipped into the deep end of the pool. I followed. Then, about fifteen others splashed in to join us. A "keep-away" water fight began immediately, with an oversized beach ball as the pursued prize. The sides were made up of natural competitors, guys versus girls! It lasted a marathon three hours! Dede appeared to be treading water for the full 180 minutes. I tried to look rugged as possible, but clutched the side of the pool, when I thought she wasn't looking. I later learned that Dede was a qualified water safety instructor, had been a lifeguard, and often performed in synchronized swimming competition.

An hour into our keep-away fun, Dede and I wrestled over the beach ball. An hour later, we were wrestling and neither had the ball! We were mutually smitten. The chemistry was immediate and complete. I know it sounds shallow, but I couldn't help but notice she was wearing a new two-piece swimsuit, something not often seen in the mid-60s. The next day I was shown a newspaper ad for the local gym, with her swim-suited photo featured as the example of how a client would look if gym attendance were regular. She had my full attention!

After the "keep-away" playfulness that lasted until 1:00 a.m., I sat in the shallow end of the pool with her alone, and she entertained me with funny spoonerisms. Spoonerisms are familiar stories, fairy tales, or poems, where consonants and vowels are purposely swapped out to delight a listener. Dede recited "Prinderella and the Prandsome Hince," and topped it off with "Paul Revide's Rear." I was fascinated as I laughed, even though I shivered in the Northern California late night air. I didn't mind the cold at all! At two in the morning, I took Dede and her saintly patient sister to a local Denny's for coffee. That is honestly how we met. Sounds almost lecherous, yes?

We dated for a year. She was working on her Master's degree

at Stanford University and I was a new elementary teacher in a small town near San Jose. We discovered that when I was eight and Dede was three, our families lived in San Mateo about two blocks from each other, but never met because my family left the neighborhood about a year before her family arrived.

I was entranced with Dee's complete naturalness and her innocent honesty. What I saw and experienced was who she really was. No pretensions—none! An example of this: on our fourth date, we mutually said we loved each other. That takes courage, because if one person does not feel that way, it can be devastating for the other. We continued to date others we had been dating because at that time, neither of us was ready for commitment. But we continued to drift closer to each other, experiencing mutual respect and admiration.

The lesson in this chapter is to be open-minded enough to say yes to invitations. If we had followed our inclination to say no to attending the party, we would never have met, never would have married, and wouldn't have had the amazing invitations you will read about in this book.

Just say yes.

## LESSON

*Be open to invitations. You never know what*
*good is already waiting for you.*

Living in Venezuela. First year as singles in bachelor
quarters and next four years as married after big wedding in
California. Yes, that is a boa constrictor around our necks.

# Chapter Two

## Invitation to Work in South America

*To those leaning on the sustaining infinite,
today is big with blessings.*

— Mary Baker Eddy

An invitation arrived for Dede from a cousin of a family friend who invited her to teach American children in a school for United States citizens in Venezuela, South America. United States Steel Corporation had established the school for children of their American employees and for other children working for other American companies.

Dede was quickly hired for one of four available teaching positions. She was told that over 400 hopeful teachers had applied and most had been interviewed in the United States by the school superintendent. Dede's new job was to be in Puerto Ordaz, a somewhat upscale suburb of newly established Ciudad Guayana. It was located on the picturesque confluence of the Caroni and Orinoco Rivers featuring the stunning Llovizna Falls. The city, constructed from scratch by American company Bechtel Engineering, was to be the location of her five-year employment with a big salary, comfortable living, and adventure. Exciting for the twenty-five-year-old Dede Davenport!

This became an even better opportunity than expected

because living expenses were low. A new house rented for fifty dollars a month, with twenty-two-cent movie nights at the country club that also provided golf, tennis courts, and pretty good food. By accepting this invitation, Dede could pay off her Stanford University loan where she had earned her Master's Degree in art education.

After Dee was hired, I applied but did it too late to be interviewed by the Superintendent who had returned to Venezuela after selecting his four needed teachers.

Since Dede would be on her way to Venezuela, I decided to see the world on my own. I applied for a position to teach children of military families in a foreign land with the United States Army. Four months after I received the rejection letter from U.S. Steel, the army offered me a position to teach American kids in Japan. The terse offer stated that I had to accept or decline within forty-eight hours of the offer. No exceptions and no extensions.

Just before the offer in Japan, I learned that one of the four originally hired teachers could not accept the job, meaning a teaching position opened in Venezuela. Before accepting the position in Japan, I wanted to be absolutely sure there was no opportunity to be with Dede in South America. We had become more serious with our relationship, and the Venezuelan position would be better in every conceivable way. With only the rejection letter received four months earlier, I intended to place a phone call. Because the town was new, I was told there was no telephone system in place at that date. I placed a call anyway, through an international telephone operator, and discovered that U.S. Steel had just completed putting in its own telephone system for company business and for contact with the rest of the world. I telephoned and the call went directly to the school superintendent. There was no forwarding.

Amazingly, I had interrupted an actual meeting where he and the school principal were choosing a replacement for the woman who could no longer accept the position. They were reviewing the original applications once more. The superintendent, surprised by the timeliness of my call, chatted with me briefly. He stated, "Even if I wanted to hire you, you are in a difficult position, because the Army is demanding an answer in only two days. Because of our company's procedures, it would take me four days to get an acceptance for you from U.S. Steel's headquarters in Pittsburg. If you want to, you can take the chance and stall Japan."

Two days later, Dede and I were enjoying dinner with her parents and their friends when my landlady telephoned. She had a telegram for me.

"Open it," I said.

Two welcome words were, "Welcome aboard!"

Apparently the superintendent had hired me without Pittsburg's authorization.

The specific company that hired us was Orinoco Mining Company, a subsidiary of U.S. Steel, so named for the immense Orinoco River that passed near an important mountain, Cerro Bolivar. Orinoco Mining, with Cerro Bolivar, was exceedingly valuable to U.S. Steel, as it was mining the mountain with the most pure iron ore in the world. Its value was placed at ten billion dollars when it was discovered in 1947, and is worth ten times that amount today. The company could afford to be generous to its employees, and so built a new town for them and paid them well. Ciudad Guyana, with a population of a few thousand when we were there in the years 1967-72, is today a city of over one million.

Dee and I drove from San Francisco Peninsula to U.S. Steel's headquarters in Pittsburg, then on to New York where her 1963 Chevy was shipped to Venezuela. Ciudad Guyana is 400 miles east of Caracas, directly below the island of Trinidad where we participated in two fabulous *Carnaval* celebrations.

Our classes in the American school sometimes had as few as eight students, and we could often work with students one to one. A teacher can work miracles with that ratio! Dede had first grade classes, averaging eight to ten students. My seventh grade classes wavered between eight and twenty-one. Most years it was on the low side, so that students could write a composition every day and read it aloud to me. We corrected and discussed it together. There was no television during the first four of the five years we were there, so American youths read everything they could find. Some of my seventh-grade students regularly read periodicals like *Time Magazine* and told me what was happening back in the States.

One thing we laughed about was the name of the school, named after an attorney, Jose Travieso, who wrote up the papers to establish the school. *Travieso* in Spanish means naughty, mischievous, needing reforming. So, Travieso School could be casually referred to as "Reform School."

Most American children could speak Spanish because all attended Venezuelan kindergarten classes before attending grades one through eight with instruction in English. Most remained somewhat bilingual because in our school, they had forty-five minutes of Spanish instruction every day. All of the students studied hard because they had to leave Venezuela and their parents after completing eighth grade. They needed to compete to get into the best private high schools in the States, and their parents had the money to pay for it. When a student had to attend a lesser school, everyone in town knew it. If the student didn't have the grades to enter a good stateside school, the Venezuelan high school might await him. Few students wanted that, so our teaching was easy because the students were motivated to do their best.

It helped that there were no single parents. Not one. Moms rarely worked and were home to guide and encourage. No dad had to commute more than three miles, so he was home about four o'clock in the afternoon. Remembering *Leave it to Beaver* or *Father Knows Best*, it was the 1960s with behavior more resembling the

50s. When the American company Kaiser came to the community to build Guri Dam, one of largest dams in the world, our kids were aghast. They said, "The kids from Kaiser smoke, and they wear *bell-bottoms!*" Our schoolkids were awfully sheltered and clearly wholesome.

On Valentine's Day, 1968, I proposed to Dede. Then that summer, we went to California to marry. Dede Davenport became Dee Gruenig. Dede was too hard for her girlfriends to say, when combined with the Swiss German name of Gruenig, so they began calling her Dee and I did too.

We shipped new furniture from the States to fill our new two bedroom, one bath house featuring a large combination living room with dining area. A spacious, well-equipped kitchen with large pantry completed the house. Finally, a fenced-in yard with grass, trees, numerous iguanas, and other assorted harmless animals made up the yard.

We took a daily noon nap in an air-conditioned bedroom, considered a tangible luxury because our home, and almost all homes, had only oversize windows with plantation louvers to let air pass through for cooling. To complete our family, we had a half-German Shepard dog, two parrots, and a lovable sloth named Herbie. The sloth had the run of the house and was not allowed outside because he would head for the nearest treetop and we would lose him. However, we did take him into the yard for sloth races against two other sloths, owned by American friends, with a tall front yard tree being the coveted finish line. Running a ten-yard race at top sloth speed could take about twenty minutes. Going on about Herbie would take a couple of chapters, if not an entire book, so his adventures will go into a blog with the website address being the title of this book. Now, to get back to the subject of Dede.

We loved everything about the five-year adventure. We explored Venezuela, traveled through the rest of South America, and experienced most of Europe during the summers. We had accepted invitations to teach American children in a foreign land but we experienced so much more. We enjoyed the wider experience of living in another culture that was vastly different from comfortable and familiar California. With no telephones in the home, friends dropped in to chat. With no television, our first four of five years, dinner parties and social bridge were popular. Life was spontaneous, friendly, and comfortable. Today we remain good friends with Americans and others who shared our adventures. We still occasionally travel abroad together almost fifty years later.

The good times in Venezuela were about to end.

Our lovable pet sloth, Herbie, who could beat other sloths in races. A race with a distance of ten yards would take twenty minutes at Herbie's top speed.

## LESSON

*When you are told there is no chance, no possibility, take action anyway. Pick a belief system that serves you.*

# Chapter Three

## Invitation to Accept Two Jobs With One Interview

*Wake up to what has already been provided.*

— Beca Lewis, Living in Grace

In 1972, the nationalization of the Orinoco Mining Company, the subsidiary of U.S. Steel for which we worked, was imminent. There would be big changes in the country that would affect our town and our American expatriate school. Though we personally heard nothing said to us by the local populace, graffiti on the walls shouted, "The iron ore is ours!"

We made the decision to return home.

Teaching positions were virtually non-existent in California. Arriving home, we relocated to Southern California instead of the Bay Area, because now we were used to the warm weather. We drove through Los Angeles, Orange, and San Diego Counties looking for work. Due to California's budget crises at that time, teachers were being pink-slipped in droves. Neither of us could get a single application for a teaching position in any school district in Orange or Los Angeles counties. Not one! We tried for several weeks during the summer of our return in 1972.

Besides looking for a job, I attended classes at the University of Southern California. I completed my school administration credential that I had begun during previous summer recesses, living in a USC dormitory, when we were not traveling elsewhere. One day, my university advisor telephoned, "Quick, jump in your car and drive to Ramona. A teaching position just became available!"

Immediately, Dee and I left to drive south through farmlands and orchards to arrive in the little town of Ramona. On the way, we saw few people and even fewer cars. Dee wondered out loud, "Who could find this remote place?" Yet, we hoped an opportunity might be promising.

Upon arriving, an elderly gentleman shuffled out of a small shack that served as the district office. What he told us was difficult to believe. He said that forty candidates had already appeared for that one job that very day. I am not sure I believed forty, but clearly other candidates had arrived before us. After six weeks, we still had not been given a single application to teach anywhere and were willing to give bilingual education a try in East Los Angeles. Even that had no openings.

We didn't panic. The drive through beautiful Southern California each day was enjoyable. Dee and I had fun, quietly listened for guidance, and expected success to be waiting in the right location at the right time.

Eventually, we noticed a small sign over an old trailer on an empty road near newly forming Mission Viejo. It read: A Saddleback Valley Unified School District is being established by combining San Joaquin Elementary and Tustin High School Districts. We parked our car and went inside. Two friendly women greeted us and we began an animated conversation. We easily connected with them, chatting and laughing as we shared our adventures in South America.

The next day, I received a phone call at USC to appear for a job interview. It came from one of the two women who identified herself as the superintendent's secretary for the soon-to-be-combined school districts. She invited me to a Mission Viejo elementary school to interview for a teaching position. I had no idea how she found me sixty miles north in Los Angeles. I didn't know her identity at the time, but must have given her my contact information.

I interviewed, but didn't think I interviewed particularly well. The interview lasted an hour and a half, ending on the first base side of the school's baseball diamond. Oddly, I blurted out something with no foundation at all, suggesting there might be a chance of a job for Dee in some other remote school district. I have no idea why I said that, as there was absolutely no other job opportunity that I knew about. As I said it, the interviewer was looking down at the ground, not looking at my face, and he interpreted my comment as fact.

He intoned, "What you are saying, Mr. Gruenig, is that we need to hire both of you or hire neither of you."

With mouth wide open but unable to speak, I tried to say, "No, that is not what I am saying!"

Too late! He spun on his heels and walked rapidly from the diamond to the administration office. I strained to keep up with him. He phoned what was then called Personnel Resources, saying, "I want to hire someone and I want a job for his wife."

Amazingly, though I hadn't told him much about Dee, we both were hired on the spot, with only my interview, even though neither of us had submitted an application. Dee's future principal accepted her on his teaching staff without ever meeting her. Her interview consisted of him saying, "I can give you a choice of kindergarten or second grade."

This was astounding, because we learned later that Dee's principal was a politically powerful administrator, well known to be fussy about who worked at his school. A flamboyant individual, he would introduce his teachers at school district meetings as being the best in the district. Most of his teachers were young and attractive, two had won beauty contests, and collectively he called his school location "Fox Hill." The widely circulated joke was that he hired his teachers with a tape measure. In reality,

I am certain he normally interviewed each candidate carefully before hiring, but not that time, not with Dee whom he accepted without seeing or speaking with her.

Neither the jobs in Venezuela or in California could have been planned by Dee or me, though it would be wonderful to claim credit for how "shrewd and clever" we were. We cannot claim such credit. We believed it was the result of prayerful and expectant listening to God's omnipresent loving guidance, available to anyone who accepts it and is willing to act on it. I think that many people receive great ideas and invitations but do not trust them or act upon them. Dee did trust and act, and did it with an unstoppable passion. This pattern and practice will increasingly be shown throughout this book.

In 1978, Dee discovered a little art tool that would fascinate her for more than thirty years. At the wholesale trade show, the San Francisco International Gift Fair, she discovered art rubber stamps. They were not polymer stamps for business needs that would print "fragile" or "payment due." Art stamps sported designs and pictures of objects representing literally anything, etched deeply into a piece of red rubber, with the etched rubber placed on a cushion atop a wooden block. The images, created by putting inks directly on the rubber and then pressing the rubber to paper, could be combined to create artful scenes or an original greeting card or amusing messages on notes. They could also establish original wrapping paper, artwork for use in a handmade scrapbook, and many other entertaining things. Images etched into the rubber were funny or cute, some were edgy or weird, others beautiful. Dee preferred the beautiful images with a clean, contemporary look.

Art rubber stamps went from something unknown to over-the-top popular, because a surprisingly number of women wanted to create something original and artful. Most of them had a sense of color, arrangement, or design. Most had talent but found drawing to be the challenge. A stamp, with an image they liked but could not draw, permitted images of objects when used with first-rate inks. Then they could employ the skills that came easily to them, such as combining stamped images into themes of their own art preferences.

Dee had never seen rubber stamps before, and she was fascinated. She bought a few because she thought they would be interesting to students in her class. They certainly were! When she stamped something on a child's corrected paper, others wanted something stamped on their papers as well.

We were grateful for the teaching positions in brand-new schools. I had excellent professional support and soon became an elementary school principal, championed by the school principal who had given me the interview on the ball field. Dee had moved from her original school to a different new school with a principal she loved and a talented staff. Life seemed ideal, but somehow the time had come for Dee to try something new, something that would lead to a new career with adventure. Fifteen years later, her new career would pull me in as well.

## LESSON

*Never give up. Success just might take longer. Accept and trust that what is right for you is in place already. It will come to you or you will find it.*

# Chapter Four

## Invitation to Enter a World
## Beyond Public School Teaching

*Whatever you can do, or dream you can do, begin it. Boldness has genius, power and magic in it.*

— W. H. Murray, Scottish Himalayan Expedition

At the time of Dee's discovery of rubber stamps, a unique and special invitation arrived to introduce her to a world much wider than the public school classroom, and it didn't involve rubber stamps.

It came in the person of interior decorator Lee Mink, who was respected for superior work including outstanding decor of Occidental Petroleum's headquarters in Los Angeles prior to the headquarter's move to Houston. This was the well-known sixteen-story Armand Hammer building in Los Angeles. Lee completed the innovative decor for Mr. Hammer's personal offices and the top two floors.

Dee took one of Ms. Mink's interior design classes. Dee loved it so much that Lee invited her to teach, specializing in the area of color that was to become Dee's specialty. This made it possible for her to get a resale license, so that as a side activity, she could design the interiors of some friends' homes.

Dee preferred to save her friends money by encouraging them

to keep furnishings they had, and then add accessories she had chosen to tie everything together. She always interviewed each friend carefully, to understand who they really were, and what would make their home especially inviting and comfortable. Friends noticed her accessory choices, liked them, and asked her to purchase something the same or similar. Acquiring accessories for gifts for friends and clients soon became a small business called Posh Presents with an inviting "posh collection" of items perfect for gift-giving.

## LESSON

*Be willing to learn something new. You*
*never know where it will lead.*

# Chapter Five

## Invitation to Build a Home Party Business

*It is not how much you do but how much love*
*you put into the doing that matters.*

— Mother Teresa

An invitation was extended by a neighborhood friend to show the "Posh Collection." It was an assortment of items suitable for Christmas holiday gift giving, made up of accessories she had provided to interior design customers. A neighbor invited Dee to show the collection to a group of forty friends in her home. After a sumptuous dessert, Dee showed the collection, one item at a time, to guests sitting in a wide double circle. The potential gifts were presented in the same order as they were printed on a list. The list was beautifully printed on the highest quality card stock, much like a menu at a fancy restaurant. Enveloping the menu was a charcoal gray cover with her Posh Presents Inc. logo in sparkling silver.

As each item appeared from its cloth enclosure, all made by Dee's mother, guests were encouraged to write directly upon the list their notes what they thought of each item. Also, they were encouraged to write who might enjoy receiving each as a gift. Dee loved to show how each gift item could be used. After showing each one, she passed them around for everyone to hold and examine. After showing a hundred items the first summer, she later trimmed them down to sixty-five to make it more manageable. Most participants wrote copious notes on the lists. By handling the items and writing about them, guests tended to make each one their own. The enveloping cover made everything look classy, and the collection appeared more expensive than it was. The list was kept by the guests, with their written notes personalizing it. They showed it to friends after the home party and this comprised the most potent advertising imaginable.

Emphasis at the party was upon enjoyment and fun. Sales took care of themselves in a natural, low-key flow. Purchases were paid for that evening, for delivery to our home in early December. She had thoroughly researched which companies were known for responsible on-time delivery and she worked only with those companies.

The home party concept worked exceptionally well because Dee wisely paid attention to which party guests were most enthusiastic, and which made the largest purchases. As there were more guests that wanted to host home gatherings than Dee had time to accommodate, she chose only the most passionate guests to host their own home party gatherings.

Sales began in June and continued until she returned to the classroom in September. During this three-month period, sales at each evening's presentation increased so much that August's sales blew past sales in June. The word got around, from friend to friend, and with practice, Dee improved, becoming an excellent presenter. The bank balance kept growing.

A friend of mine who knew that Dee was out late into the evenings, asked me about her "late night profession." Barely amused by the question, I only winked.

From 1979 until 1983, while still teaching public school, Dee continued with home gatherings during the summer months. When fulfilled orders from manufacturers arrived at our home in early December, she, with a crew of girlfriends and neighbors, packaged the items for customers. During that time, I had trouble finding an opportunity to shower and dress, and was timing my dashes around the house filled with busy women.

Dee and her friends put the gifts into crisp, oversized, pure white bags set off with a lovely, wide lavender ribbon attached to one of the handles. After delivery, the bags, stuffed with what customers had chosen and previously paid for, covered a large section of the host's living room floor. The delight for Dee was watching the excited host call friends and guests to pick up their orders. Sometimes it seemed like a second party.

After the first year of doing the home gatherings alone, Dee added six more friends to schedule and work their own home party gatherings.

In 1983, we both thought that 1984 might be a tough year for home gathering parties because the 1984 Summer Olympics were coming to Los Angeles. We thought that Olympic traffic would make it nearly impossible for guests to get to gift selection parties. Therefore, she discontinued them, which turned out to be unnecessary because Olympic Organizer Peter Ueberroth was so proficient. With him at the helm, Los Angeles and Orange County traffic flowed better than it had in years!

Overall, home gatherings were successful because they stretched Dee's presentation abilities and led to future opportunities. With them, Dee built a foundation of devoted, enthusiastic customers who continued to follow her progress in the years to come.

A new invitation arrived, this one from a large, respected fund-raising organization. To complete the transition, Dee's little Mazda sedan that had served her well for getting her collection to home parties fizzled, to show it was time to leave the gatherings in homes behind.

Immediately after purchasing a more substantial Toyota van, we watched the salesman who made the sale get into the little compact to drive it to another place on the lot. Though it had never given any trouble, suddenly it wouldn't start. Then smoke billowed from under the hood. This seemed to be confirmation that Dee and Posh Presents were ready for a new chapter with less driving all over Orange County.

After leading home parties alone in 1979, she added friends to expand the very beginnings of her business. They were Dee, Debbie, Bobbie, Barbara, and Bobbie.

## LESSON

*Be an entertainer with your work. Interact and lead. These can be learned. Few are "born" with these abilities.*

# Chapter Six

## Invitation to Thrive with a Prestige Fund-Raiser

*"If we don't change, we don't grow. If we don't grow, we are not really living. Growth demands a temporary surrender of security."*

—Gail Sheehy

**H**ome gatherings were no longer needed after a prestige invitation came from an organization we didn't know existed. These unexpected invitations from individuals or groups we were unfamiliar with continued, typical of what appeared through Dee's trustful listening and expectation of God's guidance that she believed anyone could tap into.

This invitation was offered to experience something called The Christmas Company, a classy fund-raiser for the Orange County California chapter of Junior Leagues International. JLI is a nonprofit organization of 293 Junior Leagues, located mostly in the big cities of the United States, Canada, Mexico, and the United Kingdom. It was established in 1901 by Mary Harriman, a nineteen-year-old debutante, to help immigrants in New York City. Today, each Junior League raises money to help its own community.

Each chapter raised funds in its own chosen way. Some, including the Orange County chapter, invited successful retail stores around the country known for unique, rarely seen merchandise. The fortunate stores that were chosen paid a fee for a booth and donated a percentage of what they earned to the League. With the organization coming from a debutante background in New York, the League women were sharp, well educated, and impressive.

In 1983, when Dee participated in her first Christmas Company event, about 20,000 women attended. They were voracious spenders. They attended with an intent to purchase because they expected to find unusual items for holiday gift giving and they knew that profits went to their chosen local charities. Because participating stores sold items seldom seen anywhere before, it was perfect for Dee because few had ever seen a rubber stamp.

With many people in attendance, demonstrations of rubber stamp art drew large curious crowds. Because this was something new to Dee, for this first show she hired respected stamp artist Kat Okamoto. She was known for making rubber stamping understood and wanted. Then, Dee did this for the next sixty-some shows over an eight-year period.

Dee, surprised and honored to be chosen to have a booth in the show, did not have a store, as other participants did. Though she was known for the Posh Collection of accessories for the home, the League wanted her to sell *only* rubber stamps. Some of the women who had attended Dee's home party gatherings were Junior Leaguers, and they believed that rubber stamps would be a big hit for their fund-raiser. Indeed they were, for in the first year of participation her little crowded booth sold $30,000 of rubber stamps in only twenty-nine hours, establishing an Orange Country Junior League record. She broke that record the following year with over $32,000 in sales. Though the League had a limit of three years of participation in order to keep merchandise fresh and seldom seen, Dee was invited for nine consecutive years, with sales not breaking records of her first two years, but remaining strong. The key to success was continually demonstrating what rubber stamps could ably do for those that used them. Dee showed through animated demonstrations what attendees could create and she made it look easy to do. Each greeting card or bookmark had the recipient's name placed with captivating calligraphy that is Dee's specialty.

Her early participation at Orange County Junior League fund-raiser called The Christmas Company. It was huge fun and a sales record was set two years in a row. She was invited back nine consecutive years.

She usually had large crowds watching, which was surprising because viewers couldn't see much if they were not up close to her. When she had to use the restroom, and didn't want the crowd to disperse, she would ask me to sit in. Sometimes I would say aloud for the benefit of the crowd, "But I am not an artist!"

She would then smile and place a sign around my neck that said, "If he can do it, anyone can!" It always received a laugh.

The experience with the Junior League opened a door to have an adventure in actual retailing, a gift store that sold items similar to the Posh Collection. Sales of rubber stamps were included in a small section of the store. An advantage was having a talented and creative staff right from the beginning, with Junior Leaguers as part of it. Their presence, excitement, and widespread friends brought an abundance of customers into the store.

## LESSON

*Never be intimidated by money, fame, or talent in others. Observe and learn.*

# Chapter Seven

## Invitation to Have a National Award-Winning Store

*Service we render others is the rent we pay for our room on earth.*

— Wilfred Grenfell

*Always give more than expected.*

— Linda Risbrudt

That first year with the Christmas Company holiday fund-raiser proved to be a profitable success. Dee invested her earnings into Posh Presents, a retail store in Laguna Niguel, California. Dee hired employees based upon their character, an ability to relate to the customer, and their inventiveness with an ability to have fun. Besides gifts and rubber stamps with accessories for them, creative invitations, posters, banners, parties for kids and adults, and fifty varieties of how-to classes were provided. The classy invitations to all kinds of events did well because Laguna Niguel had numerous social gatherings during the 1980s with its strong economy. These were social gatherings such as dinner parties in homes of customers, and not the social gathering parties where Dee used to show the Posh Collection.

At its opening, the store probably sold the only available rubber stamps in Orange County, and Dee had just about every brand of rubber stamp ever made. They sold exceptionally well and stampers drove substantial distances to get them. Dee encouraged staff's suggestions, inventiveness, and let them run with their ideas. This resulted in a team working together creatively in a store filled with fun for both staff and customers.

February of 1984. Opening day at Posh Presents, Dee's first store. It sold gifts, stationery, stickers, and rubber stamps.

With her first store, Dee was on fire with enthusiasm. But, an important decision, a risk, needed to be taken in support of it. On-site leadership was needed, and Dee did something most would consider completely unwise. At the Christmas holiday break, she resigned from public school teaching, at a time when she was at the top of the salary schedule. It was December, 1983 and in six short weeks, she had opened Posh Presents, just in time for St. Valentine's Day.

Dee had enjoyed teaching kindergarten, but even more, she loved art and enjoyed producing and teaching it in the store's classroom using rubber stamps, her personal specialty. She left much of the merchandising of gifts to the staff. Using the skills learned in teaching, she instructed customers in such a way that they were successful and enthusiastic about their artistic success *before* she sold them stamps and accessories. Customers found they could successfully create their own original art, make greeting cards, scrapbook pages, wrapping paper, and even decorate furniture. Dee held classes full to capacity every day with twenty-two students attending each class, and a waiting list of hopefuls. Most of the time there were two, even three classes in a day. When customers understood how to do something and were excited to get started, sales were huge.

One thing I respected about Dee was that she could stand back and let others shine. The local ABC Television affiliate asked to film a *"Mommy and Me"* class where mothers and young daughters made projects together. The television crew included actress and consumer reporter Inez Pedroza. Instead of leading the activity herself, Dee asked a talented staff member to lead the classroom activity. It appeared on the afternoon news, that same day, with both news anchors reporting it at length.

Though Dee had no formal business plan and no experience with retailing, except selling our furniture and car when leaving Venezuela, she directed the business operations and accepted continuous invitations and suggestions to put innovation into the store. The store was different, and even competitors came to see what was accomplished for customers with her creative team. She was so enthusiastic that nearly everything worked, and worked well from the beginning.

The store was located in a small, one-block shopping center nicknamed "Teacher's Row," earning its name because half of the stores were owned by former schoolteachers. There were no familiar chain stores in the small center and that made the little center special. Though somewhat hidden, the one single block was upscale, modern, and well maintained.

Posh Presents was crammed to overflowing with inviting merchandise and the front wall was all plate glass. Because the retail space was small, people passing by saw customers and associates compressed inside something like the first day of a 75% off sale at Macy's. Ten customers in the store made it seem *packed* with shoppers, with a look and feel like today's Apple computer stores. Women were lured by the apparent crowds to see what was going on. Men were smart and stayed away.

Because she had hosted four years of home parties before opening the store, Dee had accumulated a list of over 2,000 dedicated customers, actually fans, who had made large and repeated purchases at Posh Presents Parties over the years. Now they didn't need to wait for a summer's home gathering. They *piled* into the store.

Posh Presents sported a luxurious, contemporary look. Much of the original appearance was established by creative team member Linda Risbrudt, who personally represented class and beauty. Rubber stamps, manufactured by about 100 different manufacturers, needed only fifteen percent of the retail space, but they represented fifty percent of the sales. Displayed directly behind the counter were fifty colorful rolls of stickers from Mrs. Grossman's Paper Company. Stickers on rolls had just been invented by Mrs. G, and it seemed that most customers wanted to purchase several strips of them. Andrea Grossman told us that Posh Presents sold more of her stickers than any store in the world. It pays to be early and first with something.

Laguna Niguel was a fairly wealthy Orange County town. Posh Presents attracted two different types of customer. Half of them shopped dressed to the nines and wearing four-inch pumps. They purchased the gifts. The other half loved rubber stamps and made all kinds of artful projects for friends that they learned in Dee's classes. They shopped casually, wearing shorts and sweats with tennis shoes or sandals. They bought only stamps and stamp accessories. Both groups were so different and both were appreciated and treated as special friends.

*Fun is good.*

— Dr. Seuss

First store, called Posh Presents in Laguna Niguel, was an innovative store that led to invitations for future stores. Many original artistic things were created for customers' parties and entertaining. Betty Waldeck amazed people with her talent.

Dee and her store associates loved to have fun. That kept them loose, happy, and involved with customers. One attractive team member looked like Dolly Parton. When she was a little girl, her grandfather nicknamed her his little "Dolly" when he bounced her on his knee. She served as our on-site bookkeeper, and team members playfully but respectfully called her Mother Superior.

Once, to honor her and have fun, the staff of about a dozen dressed in homemade nun habits. They had a full dinner in the stock room, decorated with fake stained glass windows and the whole cathedral ambiance. Though we had no clue about any team member's religious affiliations, that evening everyone was a good Catholic. Of course Dolly sat in proper costume at the end of the table, as our Mother Superior.

Posh had not only innovation for customers, but innovation with fun as well. One evening all staff in our first store became nuns to honor the store's bookkeeper they called "Mother Superior."

For some, Posh Presents became a home away from home. One team member was in the process of leaving her husband. She parked her car blocks away when working, so that he wouldn't find and confront her. But one morning, when making the actual move, she parked directly in front of the store. He saw her car and having a spare key, unlocked it, opened her suitcase, and threw her clothing all over the parking lot. She hid behind the sales counter as I blocked the door to prevent him from coming in after her. I wasn't sure what I would do if he tried to enter because he displayed a full head of steam. Happily, he didn't try to get in and abruptly left. His actions that day confirmed her decision because they permanently parted.

For at least one other team member, the store provided a place of safety. One employee spent some entire nights in the store to escape domestic abuse by her husband.

Fortunately, many little things regularly occurred to get laughs and to keep it light. Once, after designing a new website, I temporarily linked it to the Nordstrom shoe department for their first viewing. The all-female staff loved it!

Store staff had good self-images. Once, I came in the back door calling to Dee, "Hey, Gorgeous!" I believe that every team member turned and looked my way, certain that I was speaking to them. One even came in from an adjoining room!

The principal reason the store did well was because Dee and her team went out of their way to make the store different from other stores for their customers. She and two staff members often flew to the East Coast to seek the newest and best products, including attending the New York Stationery Show, so that California customers would always find new items at her store.

Posh Present's gift-wrap was all original. No pre-prepared bows were used. Ms. Risbrudt taught everyone on staff how to wrap for gift giving from scratch. Customers brought gifts purchased at some competing stores for Posh to wrap, and so beautiful packages were sent far beyond Dee's Laguna Niguel store. At least one went to the Queen of England.

Staff regularly attempted creative projects for customers that even staff had not seen done before. Most involved challenging stationery and paper projects, to do something completely original and new. When staff was not 100% successful at doing anything innovative, there was no charge to the customer. The creative team had to continually learn from successes and failures because they had no precedent to copy. Fortunately, failures were few and successes were numerous, so that Orange County passed the word around. The good results were trumpeted in local newspapers and magazines.

Posh's "home made" gift wrap of white glossy paper that was rubber stamped was chosen to be the first full color photo placed into *RubberStampMadness*, the first and original magazine for rubber stamping.

Posh Presents was more successful than we could have hoped for. In 1993, *Gifts and Decorative Accessories* magazine, the leading magazine for the gift industry, invited Posh Presents to participate in their national competition for distinction in merchandising achievement. The store, with its strong staff, won a national second place. Then in 1999, Dee was selected by the Los Angeles Gift Mart as Retailer of the Year.

Another national magazine, *Gifts and Stationery Business*, published a six-page color feature about Posh Presents and compared the city's four leading gift stores with it. Posh came out on top. Our store manager, Kimberly Begin, who was largely responsible for earning the Gifts and Decorative Accessories award, graced GSB's front cover.

What really made the store click? Under-promising and over-delivering to the customer! Dee liked to surprise and delight. While competing gift stores had one or two associates on the floor, Posh had four to six to ensure rapid, efficient service. The large staff was especially necessary when the store had an average of two classes almost every day. Each class released twenty-two potential customers into the small retail space. Customers looking for rubber stamps and other materials used in the classes needed help to quickly locate them. This was expensive for us, but it kept customers happy and the store full of excitement. In addition, the bright, wholesome team members attracted other employees like them. Two had worked in Disneyland. One had been Alice on the "Alice in Wonderland" float for Disney's Electrical Parade float and another had played Snow White in costume when she was eighteen.

Kimberly Begin, manager of the first store. It won second place in a nationwide contest for Outstanding Achievement in Store Design.

Once, when we had a new outstanding store manager, her first day on the job happened to coincide with the day of a Tony Robbins total day motivational seminar. Dee suggested, "Let's take her with us!" What a kickoff for that first day that set in place the can-do attitude for our new store leader. Dee liked to do things like that. I did too.

Friends Barry and Gayle Ackerman provided an additional dimension for the store. They led stamping retreats for those who could not get enough stamping. They organized and led the first one to fascinating Catalina Island. As the song goes, it really is twenty-six miles off the California coast.

There were challenges. Occasionally something happened that baffled Dee, who searched for a solution. One woman attended many Posh Presents classes and during each class, she would boldly stand up and take photos or notes of each step of projects being taught. The projects were original, special, with much time devoted to preparation. Dee and her staff wanted to tell the woman to stop, but curiously, no one did. Then, to make everyone really concerned, the woman opened a store about twenty miles away and named it Classy Presents, a name so similar to Dee's store Posh Presents. Further, Classy Presents sometimes had its store windows decorated just like Posh Presents on Monday mornings after the woman had taken weekend classes in Dee's store!

What made it difficult to tell her to stop was that she became one of Posh's best customers. "What should we do with such an 'in-your-face' problem?" asked Dee.

No one spoke up, but saying nothing turned out to be the best response, because the woman remained a best customer and soon approached Dee to be a sincere, trusted friend. A forgiving Dee welcomed her friendship and almost immediately learned that all of this copying was the woman's admiring desire to create a store like Dee's as a gift for her daughter. After a short time, the new store closed because the daughter had no real interest in it.

Instead of an unsettling altercation, Dee and the woman remained good friends and enjoyed each other's company for years.

Some publicity the store received amazed and puzzled us. The local weekly newspaper, the *Laguna Niguel News,* had a four-column front page. Once, the paper published a feature about Posh Presents, with a photo of Dee sitting on the floor surrounded by rubber stamps. The photo covered nearly half of the front page. The story of the store filled three of the four columns. A rare murder in our peaceful community was reported with a tiny photo of the victim in only one column. Go figure!

The word got around. The write-ups in local and national magazines led to invitations for Dee to open stores in prestigious shopping centers. This presented yet another opportunity for Dee to call upon inner guidance for the right decisions.

♡
## LESSON
*Surround yourself with winners, people who have talents that you may not have. Give credit for what they do and be proud of them.*

# Chapter Eight

## Invitation to Extend the Home Base of Innovation

*Change is inevitable. Progress is optional.*

— Tony Robbins

*It's amazing how much can be accomplished if no one cares
who gets the credit.*

— John Wooden

With the reporting of the first store's success in local newspapers and national trade magazines, Posh Presents was invited to have not only one, but two temporary stores in prestigious South Coast Plaza Mall. This huge shopping mecca was, and is, considered to be the best shopping center in the western United States. South Coast Plaza is top of the line, completely upscale. Most retailer tenants there have nationally known chains of over a hundred stores. When Dee was invited, some retail chains could not get tenant space. Dee had one little store in Laguna Niguel, yet she was invited to be with the major players. The invitation was only for temporary Christmas stores but it was *South Coast Plaza!*

Dee was walking on air to have a presence there. The

invitation was a complete surprise because we knew no one affiliated with the prestigious mall. Neither she nor I would have had the gumption to ask for a tenant space, not when we were new with limited experience and a short track record. Dee could have said no, as a store with expensive rent located there could suffer irreversible losses. She said her usual yes.

Dee's decisions were sometimes discussed with me, but especially in the beginning, invitations and decisions came only from her own prayerful listening. Call it intuition if you must. Call it The Source. Call it what you will, but for Dee's thirty-year career, her listening with trust, and then taking enthusiastic action with complete dedication worked. It still does.

Now, she and her staff set out to see how they could make this big leap successful. One nice surprise was that rent for these two temporary stores was lower than for our little first store. Possibly that was because South Coast Plaza invited Dee instead of her asking to be there. With the low rent the Plaza offered, it was affordable, even with the expensive common area maintenance charges that every tenant must pay.

Since the invitation from SCP was to sell only rubber stamps, we decided to call the two temporary stores Posh Impressions, instead of Posh Presents. Two reasons for the change of name; stamps could *impress* someone the first time demonstrated, and they also produced an image, an impression on a paper or other surface. Therefore, it made sense to use the new name for stores specializing only in rubber stamps. The stores were supported by animated demonstrations-driven sales. One store was placed on the first floor of SCP's Crystal Court wing, and the other store was adjacent to Nordstrom on the third floor, that floor featuring only specialty stores for the holidays. It shared a common wall with Nordstrom and there was an amazing, amusing coincidence.

Posh Christmas party with stores' combined creative teams

A year earlier, when kidding around, I had a fake newspaper made at Knott's Berry Farm. The headline, in big bold letters announced, "Posh Presents Buys Nordstrom!" With a grin, I told our staff, "Okay, gang, get busy and make it happen!" Just for laughs, I posted it in the customer's restroom.

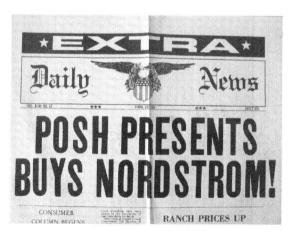

Newspaper with headline joke printed earlier, it later became true
when two letters removed from in the word "buys" became "by"
because Posh Impressions was placed next to Nordstrom. It shared
a common wall in the holiday store section of South Coast Plaza.

After signing the lease, I made changes to the displayed headline. In the word "buys," I crossed out the letters "u" and "s" so that it read, "Posh Presents *By* Nordstrom!" We always tried to keep the business light and have fun.

After Christmas, the temporary store adjacent to Nordstrom for the holidays closed down. It had enjoyed a four-month run from September through Valentine's Day. Then Dee was given the invitation to make the store in the Crystal Court side of South Coast Plaza *permanent.* Its tenant space was just right for her. It was large and had hardwood floors that felt and sounded terrific. A group of shoppers made the atmosphere sound like the invasion of a buffalo herd. It had convenient parking located directly beneath the store with a luxurious elevator to take customers one story up to our ground-level store.

Jay Leno surprised our Posh staff by picking up a large package from the display window in our South Coast Plaza store.

Best of all, the spacious plate glass front window could feature a member of our staff demonstrating the making of rubber-stamped greeting cards. We had her sit on a slightly elevated "window stage" with her back to the window. People passing by could then look over her shoulder and thereby watch her stamp items "right side up." Also, window shoppers *outside* the store saw the delighted, laughing faces of those *inside* the store directly watching the demonstrator. Next, many window shoppers came into the store to see what was happening and to join in the fun.

Posh Impressions' sales soared in South Coast Plaza. Based upon the standard measurement of sales per square foot, Posh was tenth in sales in the less busy Crystal Court side of SCP, and first of three stores in its category of stationery and gifts. Going into this luxurious center with two stores at the same time was a courageous thing for Dee to do. She and I had to dismiss any fearful thoughts, do our homework, and be successful, thankful to be there.

After several years, we learned that rent for this permanent store in South Coast Plaza's Crystal Court would become much more expensive. We decided to make a change. As we were now a known destination and didn't need curious "walk-bys" that a mall can provide, we wanted a place that would provide reasonable rent. We didn't accept an offered eight-year lease at SCP's Crystal Court because after ten years of the popularity of rubber stamps, they were beginning to slip. If the slide continued, an eight-year lease with regular high rent could lock Dee in and ruin her. Now, rubber stamp stores were popping up everywhere and even though some of them were doing poorly with sales, new stamp stores continued to open, creating saturation. Stores in Orange County that sold stamps exclusively or in part, including big box stores like Michaels and Jo-Ann, had increased from only ours to thirty. We quickly realized that we needed to always do something fresh and new, to continually reinvent ourselves in order to stay in front. Our realization was that if no one was chasing us, we were not doing something right.

Our biggest and best competitor, Stampa Barbara, had a legendary rubber stamp store in Santa Barbara. They were *so* popular that we heard stories of rubber stampers on the East Coast flying to Los Angeles and renting a car to drive north two hours to satisfy their passion. Their store was a respected wonderland of stamps. On all four walls, stamps were placed snugly into narrow shelves from the floor to an extra high ceiling. We, like others, entered Stampa Barbara to drop our jaws at their magnificent array of thousands. The store commanded respect and we gave it to them.

Stampa Barbara moved into the Crystal Court to replace our presence. Their large and beautiful store was bigger than ours had been, and likely commanded full rent, while earlier we had been fortunate to pay something affordable.

Just before we left Crystal Court, a mutually embarrassing but funny incident happened regarding Stampa Barbara and Dee. She needed to use the restroom located outside her first-floor store. For some strange reason, she instead decided to find one on the second level. Ascending the nearby stairs, she ran into the owner of incoming Stampa Barbara peering through our store's front window from the vantage point of the floor above. Both he and Dee froze in surprise. Because he clearly appeared embarrassed, Dee invited him to come down the stairs and enter the store for a tour and to ask any questions. He felt awkward about the invitation, respectfully declined, and I think he stood in the store's doorway while Dee answered a question or two.

Sadly, Stampa Barbara went out of business within a couple of years, beginning with the Crystal Court store. The most likely expensive rent and drop-off in interest in stamping probably hurt them. Also, with the establishment of their Crystal Court location, there was less of a need to drive up to Santa Barbara to shop, so it later closed as well. I say sadly because Santa Barbara created excitement to make stamping desirable, benefitting that art and craft activity for everyone. By being prudent and listening for guidance, Dee had left SCP's Crystal Court at the right time. This was one of the few times she refused an invitation when she was invited to renew.

Dee and I did not see other stores as competitors. The increased interest in stamping established a bigger pie for everyone. It was in Dee's in character to assist others if she could. Dee's belief was, "What you put out there comes back to you." It was the way she lived her life. I think that was true for us both. Because she respected other stamp and scrapbooking stores, they often invited Dee to demonstrate and teach classes for a fee. Like our stores, classes provided the engine for their sales because classes instilled understanding and a desire to purchase. Since Dee was being paid well to do this, she felt that she had a responsibility for the store to have the biggest day of sales they had ever had. Sometimes she could make it happen.

While pondering the acceptance of an eight-year lease extension beyond our existing lease for South Coast Plaza, Dee received an invitation to open a temporary retail holiday space from a mall in Brea. The Brea Mall was busy and successful in Orange County, second only to South Coast Plaza in customer traffic and sales. It also featured the best-known stores that pulled in customers from all over the county. When Nordstrom moved in, and a big parking structure was built for the occasion, the entire mall advanced a notch higher.

Unlike South Coast Plaza, there was only one empty tenant space in the popular Brea Mall. We both didn't know a single thing about the small city of Brea and had never been there. We live near the beach and Brea is ninety minutes north and inland from our home. When the Brea leasing agent telephoned Dee to invite her to lease that space, she declined.

When Dee told girlfriends who knew the Brea area that she had refused the invitation they couldn't believe it. They asked where the available space was located. She replied it was next to the mall's main fountain, next to Santa Claus at Christmas. "You refused? Dee, are you nuts?" they asked.

Her buddies insisted that she call back immediately and accept the offer. This was the second time she had said no to an invitation, but after listening to trusted friends, she changed her refusal into a trusting yes.

At this time, midway through her thirty-year career, Dee

asked me to leave my career of education and to join the business full time. I gladly said yes because I was catching her bug for the business and saw invitations come repeatedly.

Everything with Posh was getting to be complex with multiple stores, videos, books, television, and Dee increasingly traveling to work at stores and shows. Store managers needed guidance and we needed to be better aware of what was happening in the two stores she had at that time. New invitations and challenges were being accepted while still handling business activities from previous invitations. Fortunately, all was generally working well because we had a strong, talented staff and good store managers.

Dee often said, "My husband sees the big picture and I stamp each individual tree." Not true. I saw the big picture, but Dee continued doing what she preferred to do, not caring what the newest trends were in order to chase them. Sometimes this frustrated me, as I thought I knew what customers wanted. To a large extent, Dee made them want what *she* liked through her effervescent passion and connection with the customers. Decisions in the company were mostly hers because it was she who conceived the company and had put in the initial hard work.

There was work to be done when I joined Dee with the business. I had earlier been working with some negotiation of store leases and also contracts with manufacturers for putting Dee's designs and ideas into products. Marketing and promotion needed more attention and we were adding online sales in addition to those in our stores. We had new store managers to train and support. My handling of these tasks was appropriate because Dee needed to focus most upon having designs made for stamps hand-drawn by herself, her excellent on-site assistant Lynne Taylor, and occasionally an independent such as watercolorist Lisa Larsen. Additionally, Dee was traveling more to speak or demonstrate at conventions in and beyond the United States. Additionally, she continued to teach in our stores and in stores owned by others. Over the years, she had established over fifty classes but always needed to establish new ones to reflect the changing times. The original Laguna Niguel store had most of the classes, while stores in the malls tended to only *demonstrate* how to stamp because classroom space needed to be sacrificed for sales space.

Lynne Taylor, talented assistant, added beauty and humor to Posh Impressions stamp images.

Demonstrating for people walking by our stores was a big priority. We encouraged our demonstrators to engage the public with eye contact and friendly, spontaneous conversation. We didn't want them to try to impress customers with their artistic ability. That tended to discourage customers who were afraid they couldn't stamp and create as well. Dee knew that rubber stamping was a hands-on product. She wanted customers to *feel* like talented artists. Many of them did.

Initially, the Brea Mall store was temporary, intended for the Christmas season through Valentine's Day, but we accepted an invitation to stay another year and were extended reasonable rent. Next, we were offered a permanent tenant space in one of the five wings we knew would be undergoing reconstruction for at least a year. Before accepting that more expensive offer, I made an appointment to negotiate a space at the Brea Marketplace, located just across the street. It was a modern, attractive strip center.

Because originally we planned to stay in the Brea Mall, I was bold with my negotiations with the Marketplace. Surprisingly, they said yes to all requests. So, not expecting to accept a space at the Marketplace, and initially preferring to remain at the mall, I asked for even more and got it. Eventually the offer was way too sweet to turn down, and we moved across the street to the Brea Market Place for five years.

Brea Marketplace store. All six stores were often busy with an emphasis on fun.

It was ideal. The adjacent mall brought customers to the area but the Marketplace provided parking directly in front of the new store instead of in a huge parking lot. The new location was smaller, but just right for us. We could still fill the store with products to overflowing, having rubber stamps from the hundreds of brands available. This included our own line of Posh Impressions stamps that had expanded to an assortment of more than 2,000 hand-drawn contemporary images. This abundant selection brought shoppers into the store bolstered by a large area for a well-equipped, attractive classroom more suitable than the storeroom in our original store. The numerous classes, often filled to capacity twice a day, continued to be the engines that built interest and excitement for rubber stamps, scrapbooking, and creative projects. Unlike the South Coast Plaza and Brea Mall with room for only demonstrations and sales, the Marketplace space had enough room for stimulating classes, and that made sales even bigger.

One of the most successful general craft stores in the world, with the interesting name of Tall Mouse, was a short distance from our store in the Brea Marketplace. They did so well that they made a nearby new Michael's Crafts store close and move to a distant location. They had their extended family demonstrating and teaching throughout their busy store. They wanted to expand their rubber stamp department but offered not to do this while our store was nearby. They became valued friends and they kept their word not to expand. They even took us to their favorite restaurants for dinner several times and we were privileged to have dinner in their home.

During our five years in the Brea Marketplace, interest in rubber stamping continued to decline. We had shifted the focus for sales in our own stores to put more effort into rubber stamps, art papers, stamp pads, marking pens, greeting cards, and containers that would be sold in other stores. With our manufacturers, we coordinated the branding of Posh Impressions products, making them more sophisticated, and wholesaled them to stores in the United States and Europe. A few products that Dee had no part in creating were simply endorsed with her signature and photo.

As our rent and wages rose steadily, we believed it was time to close the Brea store and establish one an hour closer to our home with a fresh lease and lower expenses.

We chose Woodbridge Village in the city of Irvine. This sixth and last store had more limited foot traffic but enjoyed an excellent corner location with prominent front windows perfect for displays. Dee and her staff decorated the windows with colorful stamp-art examples blown up twenty-five times their original size. They were then attached to foam board and suspended from the ceiling. With the landlord's blessing, the attractive store, loaded with stamps and rolls of stickers covering every wall, sported a purple and red front entrance. *Better Homes and Gardens Crafts Showcase* magazine featured the store in fourteen consecutive full color pages, and it was an exciting experience to see this magazine nestled between People and Redbook at most supermarket checkout stands.

We promoted one strong team member to store manager. Earlier, when I had been a teacher, I had Jill in a class as a twelve-year-old junior high school student. She recorded student attendance for me during the first two minutes of my class teaching Spanish. At that time, two tough girls, who had cut class one day, demanded that she record them as present instead of absent. They said they would beat her up if she refused. She properly recorded them as absent and I learned later that the offending girls made Jill's school year a rough one. Jill kept her integrity, her dignity, and had never complained. When I learned of her character, I made a note on my calendar, six years forward, to hire her when she turned eighteen. She agreed! Within a year, she was a manager of our Irvine store.

The sixth store was featured with 14 consecutive pages in *Better Homes and Gardens Craft Showcase* Magazine. Occasionally busloads of shoppers would come to this store.

Though four of the five largest rubber stamp manufacturers were in California, interest in the Golden State was continuing to diminish. We knew our store in Irvine would be the last of our four permanent and two temporary locations, but we were aware that interest in rubber stamps was growing in other states and abroad.

At the turn of the new century, we closed the Irvine store and opened a studio in Lake Forest, about twenty minutes from our home. It had space for Dee and her staff to provide images for manufacturers of rubber stamps and some scrapbook papers. It also had plenty of warehouse space for Posh products to be available from both Posh Impressions online and our paper catalogs.

Over the thirty years, we hired over a hundred women to staff the stores, handle catalog and Internet sales, teach, demonstrate, and work in booths at consumer trade shows. Each store needed about twelve members, mostly part-timers. As with the first store, all of our associates were female, most of whom were young and attractive.

Just once, in the Brea Mall, we hired two young men as an experiment. That was like introducing two roosters into a hen house. When our manager saw what was going on in the stock room, she decided that this was not a good change and we went back to hiring only women.

While all of our stores did well financially at first, when rents were low and staff members were fresh and new, they became less profitable as wages and other expenses rose. We recognized that what worked one year did not necessarily work the next, and we continually innovated to stay ahead. From the very beginning, Dee made and sold instructional books and videos and demonstrated on television and at conventions. All this prepared us for the next big leap.

## LESSON

*New invitations will mean new challenges. New challenges
will mean opportunities for success.*

# Chapter Nine

## Invitation to Provide New Creative Products

*I skate to where the puck is going.*

— Wayne Gretsky

Licensing was like some kind of miracle. We didn't intend to do it nor did we originally understand it. We first refused, then said what we nearly always said, a grateful yes!

Licensing actually arrived as a result of Lady Bird Johnson's desire to beautify America, beginning with Texas. At our Junior League fundraiser booth in Austin, she asked for a Texas blue bonnet stamp. No one had ever made one, so Dee asked a manufacturer to make her two. That birthed the idea of Dee creating her own line of rubber stamps.

Rubber Stampede, Dee's second rubber stamp manufacturer, extended an invitation to go beyond manufacturing her designs into stamps for only our first store where she paid them a fee to make them. Instead, they wanted to pay her a generous royalty to put them in stores everywhere. They had their eye on the big box chain stores of Michael's Crafts, then with 800 stores and on their way to a thousand. Jo-Ann Stores with 1200 locations came after Michael's Crafts.

After first refusing to have her line of Posh Impressions rubber stamps in stores beyond her own first store, she quickly relented and gave her approval. Sales were immediately larger than we could ever hope to generate with our own efforts in our own limited venues. Rubber Stampede did well, and because they were abundantly in Michaels crafts stores, for one brief year they grew to be number one in the world's stamp sales over perennial first place manufacturer, PSX. Then, to everyone's consternation, Rubber Stampede stopped returning phone calls. Their bank had called in a big loan. Though many of the people who did business with Rubber Stampede lost money, Dee did not. Though she owed them money for stamps purchased for her own sales, they owed her money for her videos. Invoices were exchanged and the amounts each owed the other were conveniently about the same.

Dee and I thought All Night Media to be the most direct competitor of Rubber Stampede because they were of similar size. We respected All Night Media for their freshness, humorous themes, and creative packaging of stamps for gift and stationery stores where stamps had never been placed before. Both manufacturers had cartoon character licenses from Disney and other popular entities. ANM invited Dee to be licensed with them at a time when people were scattering from Rubber Stampede. Now she had a third manufacturer. All Night Media had actually been inviting Dee to work with them for a few years, but Dee didn't want to disrupt the manufacturing and distribution during a changeover of companies. However, inaccurate word on the street was that Rubber Stampede was bankrupt, so Dee agreed to license with the new company.

Then, Plaid Enterprises, considered by many to be the largest manufacturer in all of crafts, bought All Night Media. We were a license of ANM for only a few months and few of Dee's designs had been put into production with them when Plaid, our fourth manufacturer, produced them instead. Now, Dee had gone from licensing with one of the smallest of manufacturers, Polperro, that made stamps for the early years of her first store, to possibly the largest craft manufacturer of all. She proceeded from small to big under license by accepting invitation after invitation. None was requested, except when she asked Polperro to make some stamps for that first store. As a licensor, Dee was finding the work easier and more profitable. All Dee needed to do was to draw original designs that went into products manufactured by others, and to make personal appearances to support them. Part of the personal support was the writing of books, making instructional videos, and regular television appearances.

Humor worked well with Posh designs, especially drawings
that would become rubber stamps for Halloween.

Our next manufacturer was Uchida of America. The Japanese company manufactured a water-based pen called the Marvy Brush Art Marker. In 1979, the only way for a stamper to stamp an image in color was to stamp an image as an outline that looked like what you see in children's coloring books. The stamped images could then be "colored in" between the lines, looking simple and childlike.

Dee, being curious, picked up a Marvy pen and placed ink directly upon the rubber surface. She then pressed the stamp to the paper. Voilà! A brilliant, colored image appeared. No longer was stamping confined to black or the one color of a stamp pad. Vibrant images were now established that suggested professional full color printing. Dee's discovery changed rubber stamping forever and resulted in a license for a product other than rubber stamps! Because of their new popularity, Uchida wanted to double the variety of colors of their Marvy pens and invited Dee to select the colors and name them. Additionally, they placed her large photo and signature on every box and her signature on every pen.

Later, Uchida accepted Dee's idea to make a stamp pad, with one color graduated from lighter to darker tones. Called the Blending Blox Ink Pad, it contained four shades of one color hue in a pad that could be blended for variations of that color, producing a more realistic appearance.

Soon, Ranger Industries' owners asked to make a different licensed product for Dee. On a street corner in New York, she had seen South Koreans making posters, stylized alphabets, and art of brilliant colors using only a piece of leather inserted between their fingers. The talented artists' work was precise and controlled, though it must have been a trick to keep the piece of leather in perfect position while using it. Dee knew that doing something like this would be a major challenge for most crafters who were not professional artists.

Therefore, Dee and Ranger Industries came up with the idea of a sponge. Sponges would be easier for an amateur crafter to control than a strip of leather stuck between the fingers. After research and tests, Ranger produced an extremely dense sponge that could hold an abundance of ink without leaking or dripping before use. Ranger also manufactured inks for the sponge called Inkabilities that were made available in sets. The effects they produced were beautiful, and three instructional videos were produced to demonstrate the use of the art-producing sponge.

Paper Adventures, a company that made scrapbook papers, invited Dee to incorporate her designs into their products. She thought they made the best scrapbook papers anywhere that matched the high standards of their parent company Leader Stationers.

The license invitation that we especially prized was having Dee's designs on stickers made by Mrs. Grossman's Paper Company. Stickers on rolls, and later in packages seen in stationery, gift, and novelty stores everywhere, were Mrs. Grossman's. I am not sure she manufactured stickers before anyone else produced them but we believe she was unquestionably the best.

While Mrs. Grossman had her own artists to design her popular stickers, she still thought highly of Dee's designs and licensed them for stickers. To my knowledge, Dee was Grossman's only outside licensed artist. Packages had both the Posh Impressions and Mrs. Grossman's names on them. Full-page magazine ads showed smiling faces of both Dee and Mrs. Grossman. This was a generous tribute, as Andrea Grossman was so well-known and admired.

Something especially terrific to Dee was team-teaching with Andrea Grossman. The two instructed the combining of stamping with stickers at conventions and in one of Dee's stores.

Immediately after full-page ads appeared in magazines for Mrs. Grossman's stickers featuring Dee's designs, a surprise listing appeared. *Craftrends Magazine,* the bible for crafting, listed the top nine licensors for crafts. Mary Engelbreit, Thomas Kinkade, and Dee were three of the nine.

Dee continued to receive invitations from companies. American Traditional put Dee's designs into paper punches. Plaid Enterprises also made punches, but generously extended permission for Dee to work with American Traditional as well.

Other companies Dee worked with in more limited ways were Sailor for pastel pens, OttLite for lamps, Speedball for brayers, and provided designs for a small line of greeting cards for Marian Heath.

Her designs were sometimes used for instructional books and examples of art for other products not mentioned. The license we thought would be the colossal home run nearly became a colossal disaster for Dee's company and reputation. It proved to be the only invitation that should have been rejected and will be discussed in Chapter 18.

## LESSON

*Make it possible for others to enjoy your ideas. These can be products or systems.*

Here is the Craft and Hobby Association Fashion Show where models were challenged to wear clothing made from craft products. Dee wore a dress made of hundreds of pairs of gloves. The auditorium went totally black and then lights shot on, with Dee appearing, arms outstretched, to the gorgeous movie theme of *The Mission.*

# Chapter Ten

## Invitations to Teach and Use the Products

*If You Have Knowledge, Let Others Light Their Candles in It.*

— Margaret Fuller

Teaching had earlier been a major part of Dee's life and it became the launching pad for everything she did. As mentioned, she passionately taught classes in her own stores and in other independent stores. Students flocked to her classes because of the quality of the teaching and the word-of-mouth marketing for it. Stampers loved the hands-on approach where actual items were made. She also taught regularly at conventions, trade shows, and consumer shows where purchases could be made by the public.

Classes were important to create enthusiasm and sales for the stores. There were over 50 varieties, such as card and scrapbook making, gift wrapping from scratch and calligraphy. There were birthday parties and others such as Mommy and Me and Daddy and Daughter. Every effort was made to make everything as best as it could be, including the brochure of classes offered.

One event that could not be forgotten happened when a woman approached Dee at her convention demonstration table in Jackson, Mississippi. A woman with a heartbroken expression requested, "Make me a bookmark please."

To do it, Dee chose a rubber stamp with an image of an iris flower, and the woman began to cry.

"Oh my, what happened?" asked Dee.

"My name is Iris and I just lost my husband," the woman replied. Dee began to cry with her.

*Happiness is a state of inner fulfillment, not the gratification of inexhaustible desires for outward things.*

— Matthieu Ricard

Named for Quality, Value and Convenience, QVC is a home shopping network in six countries with sales generated from television. It featured assortments of products that worked well together, provided by manufacturers exclusively for QVC and offered less expensively than in stores. The goal was to sell an enormous volume of product within a few minutes of television time. Viewers called telephone operators who took their orders, accepted payment, and arranged for shipping.

Dee appeared on QVC only a couple of times. Sales were strong, maybe in spite of her being there. On camera, she stood next to the moderator, shoulder to shoulder, passionately showing *how* to use a collection of products. The moderator stressed, buy, buy, buy, eager to sell as much as possible in a few minutes of on-air time. Dee's presence on camera was unusual because the moderator normally appeared on camera alone, so it was hilarious to watch the two competing styles. But, that's Dee, not chasing the dollar, but preferring to have the customer understand how to be successful with her products.

The challenge for manufacturers, putting merchandise on

sale with QVC and home shopping networks similar to QVC, was that manufacturers were required to package their products differently from the way they would be seen in stores. They must do this for only the television sales appearance. This was expensive for them. Then, what did not sell was returned by QVC to the manufacturer and he, by agreement, must repackage the QVC assortment into its normal packaging.

Additionally, stores were not fond of home shopping networks because it undercut their sales due to home shopping's reduced prices. Finally, the large size of assortments offered on television hurt brick-and-mortar stores because customers had little need to shop for a while. Dee's brief appearances on QVC were only at the invitation of one of the manufacturers of her products.

As the twentieth century became the twenty-first, there was another unexpected invitation that was an honor. It was to be part of a new online website adventure called *Idea Forest* and was built around well-known Carol Duvall. She had the most-watched craft show on television, HGTV's *Carol Duvall Show*. The concept was to have a forest of ideas and projects available for the crafting public with the opportunity to interact with some of the best-known crafters in the industry. The website featured one crafting "expert" from each major craft category, such as painting, rubber stamping, and scrapbooking. At the time, rubber stamping and scrapbooking were the two most popular craft activities.

Each of the experts was to interact with the public within their craft specialty. Dee was invited to represent rubber stamping. Viewers were to make projects that each expert established on the *Idea Forest* website for them. The projects could be discussed with the expert. The concept didn't work at all. Little was asked of the participating "experts" and there were other problems. The website lasted about a year before it was either sold or given to the Jo-Ann Stores chain. There were three other websites created for crafts during the "dot com boom" and they folded their tents after a year or two as well.

Idea Forest was an internet shopping site introduced during the Dot Com Boom and Bust. One notable scrapper was chosen for each of eight craft disciplines to interact with viewers interested in a particular craft.

*Remember, you don't live in a world all your own. Your brothers are here too.*

— Albert Schweitzer

*Friendship is the source of the greatest pleasures, and without friends, even the most agreeable pursuits become tedious.*

— Saint Thomas Aquinas

Before the existence of Facebook, Twitter, and blogs, there was Club Posh. The website, established in October, 2001 was created by a webmaster so talented that the member women nicknamed him Super Matt. The webmaster established the website after one of Dee's fans wrote him a long letter of request for a website to feature what Dee was doing, shows and stores where she could be found, and information about the products made under her licensed name and products she endorsed. It was especially a place where club members placed their own work, made by rubber stamping with products that had Dee's name on them. They described how the project, usually a greeting card, was made and the results were discussed by members.

Club Posh was one of the earliest websites that included moderated and policed chats. The initial three moderators were talented and professional. Moderators who replaced them after serving a surprising number of years were as talented as those who served first. An astounding nearly 500 fans chose to join each month during the first year. Club membership could have been larger because many desired but were unable to interact with Dee. Though she was fascinated by gadgets, owning one of the first Palm Pilots and newer models of them that appeared each year, she refrained from learning to use a computer. This was because she drew images for stamps and papers only and always by hand. Staff members polished the drawings on a computer only to get them ready for mass production. Therefore, she could not participate in the website chats, post something, or interact in any way. On rare occasions, I would post an important announcement for her but moderators did it better. Another reason for non-participation was that she was often on the road or out of the country with long working days. I suppose she could have had someone post chats representing Dee, but this didn't seem like the right thing to do. Though fame seemed to pursue her, she would not chase it.

She did have fifty projects on the Posh Impressions website linked to the Club Posh site. They cannot be made today because most projects need supplies that are not available today. But what they were can be seen at PoshImpressions.com/projectsArchive.htm.

After a year, the club peaked at 5,000 and then receded because fresh ideas and new products were being introduced by other companies and individuals. Additionally, more websites were coming online and competing social media such as Facebook and MySpace were beginning.

After Dee's retirement in 2009, with Plaid no longer manufacturing Dee's Posh Impressions line of stamps, three manufacturing companies, one at a time, came forward asking to manufacture them under license. Members of Club Posh hoped there would be new, or at least reissued, rubber stamps after Dee's retirement, and I wanted them available for club members and others. Many were searching for used Posh Impressions stamps on eBay. Though the first of the three, Sunday International, had some initial success, for realistic reasons none of the three manufacturers' plans could be successfully realized. I had regrettably told club members of the bold, sincere plans of each potential manufacturer. When new or reissued stamps didn't come to pass, club members felt let down and disappointed. Each disappointment was worse than the last. Looking back, I should have remained quiet and then surprised members if the new or reissued products became a reality.

Today, the club website has been completely altered in look and content with all items identifying Dee or Posh removed. It has turned into an intimate friendship site where members are dedicated to one another. JudiKins, who has our permission to manufacturer Posh Impressions designs for those looking for them, generously keeps the site live for remaining members to enjoy.

The next invitations took Dee out of the United States and all over the world.

## LESSON

*The best way to understand something well is to teach it.*

Dee often demonstrated or taught the use of products incorporating her designs at trade shows and conventions.

Teaching and speaking on five continents was hugely exciting. South Africa was especially welcoming as this view of the partial crowd for host Joan Launspach and Dee illustrates. Earlier, Joan and Dee taught in Germany.

# Chapter Eleven

## Invitations to Teach Abroad

*Wherever you go, go with all your heart.*

—Confucius

In past years, the United States Army had Morale, Welfare and Recreation (MWR) programs at many forts and posts to boost morale and to provide a therapeutic experience for Army personnel and their dependents. The entire military community could participate in various arts and crafts activities. Military art instructors were trained to improve their skills each year.

Since trade shows were known to introduce the latest innovations in crafts, the Army sent the program manager for MWR to America's biggest trade show to search for instructors as well as new, interesting products for the military programs. The manager, a woman who recognized the growing popularity of rubber stamping, came across Dee's name and reputation. Originally, the manager was unsure that rubber stamping would be appropriate for or well received by the military. After watching Dee's videos showing her teaching methods, the MWR leader recommended that the Army invite her to train art instructors in Germany. Because Dee was the daughter of a Navy admiral, it was believed that she understood what the military needed. Five instructors were chosen to teach five different craft activities to art instructors in Germany.

The adventure soon expanded because the Army also had MWR centers throughout the United States and Korea.

Dee was sent first to Germany, and then South Korea and Hawaii. She was also sent to Fort Sill, Oklahoma, Fort Riley, Kansas and Fort Hood, Texas. South Korea was the most fascinating for Dee as she encountered a number of exciting or amusing experiences.

One happened when an American friend, who accompanied her had the given name of Kim. It seemed that half of the Korean soldiers had the name Kim since it is the most common family name in both Koreas. When Dee said, "Kim, let's go to dinner," more than several soldiers with the name Kim came running.

Another incident occurred when Dee visited Camp Casey, a post next to the 38th Parallel that separates the two Koreas. There were few women or children near that dangerous area. The day that Dee visited, a defecting North Korean pilot flew a stolen jet to the South. Of course, North Korea demanded that South Korea return the pilot and airplane. Forces of the North massed at the border for what looked like an imminent attack. Fortunately, it became an empty threat.

While at Camp Casey, Dee demonstrated rubber stamping and invited soldiers to sit down and give it a try. One of my favorite photos dispelled the Army's original concern about whether rubber stamping would be appropriate for rugged soldiers. The photo showed a massive master sergeant, the toughest of the tough, concentrating on coloring the rubber surface of a stamp with a brush-on art marker before pressing an image to paper. Clearly, Dee could get nearly anyone, even macho soldiers, to rubber stamp.

Dee felt immensely grateful for the opportunity to work with the Army's Morale, Welfare and Recreation Program, and the program manager has maintained a treasured twenty-five year friendship. Those enriching teaching experiences, with the diverse and different Army culture, increased her confidence and opened the door to accept non-military speaking and teaching invitations for conventions and stores in Germany, Great Britain, The Netherlands, Australia, New Zealand, South Africa, and Japan.

At Camp Casey, on the 38th parallel next to North Korea, it appears that Dee could get even rugged master sergeants to try rubber stamping.

*There is no key to happiness. The door is always open.*

Japanese proverb

Dee received a wonderful surprise invitation in 2005 to be the sole person to introduce American-style scrapbooking to the Japanese at the huge Japan Hobby Show. A special honor, indeed, because although she was an innovator with making scrapbooks in the craze's earliest beginnings, others were better known than Dee. She was especially excited about such an invitation because she had attended high school for one year in Hayama, in central Honshu, when her father had been stationed there after WWII.

The Japanese Hobby Show was held in the immense Tokyo Big Sight, a center that could hold several large conventions at one time. One hundred thousand people attended the show over a three-day period. To compare sizes, the biggest trade show for crafts in the United States was the Craft and Hobby Association show held in Anaheim, California, that at most drew 15,000 for a sometimes six-day show.

Here she is teaching to large crowds in Japan. It was an absolute thrill to be always remembered!

Dee took Yuko Neal, an American friend of Japanese descent, with her. She is a lovely woman who speaks perfect Japanese and English. Yuko makes the most complicated, gorgeous, and original handmade scrapbooks one would ever see, and she showed them in Dee's booth.

Dee had never used a microphone to demonstrate before, but needed one to speak to a wide expanse of Japanese in the audience at Tokyo Big Sight. After each sentence, a professional Japanese translator made Dee understood to the attendees. Because of the immense crowd, only those in front could see what Dee was actually demonstrating, but the Japanese were characteristically polite and sat with rapt attention.

One of Dee's instructional demonstrations was televised live for a popular morning program called *Zoom In*. The *Zoom In* crew, shooting the convention with a live connection to the network, entered Dee's large booth. The commentator asked her to make a scrapbook page featuring the two *Zoom In* anchors. Dee wanted to make the example page look its best, with balance, so she made it with the female anchor on top of the scrapbook page and the male anchor on the bottom, a Japanese cultural "no-no." Television monitors, placed in the booth, showed a live split screen with Dee speaking and the translator translating on one-half of the television monitor. The commentator was on the other half.

Suddenly the two part divided monitor became four! Each *Zoom In* anchor appeared in his or her own quarter-screen with Dee and the commentator in the other two quarters. The male anchor shown on the top left quarter playfully chastised the woman anchor on the top right quarter because her photo "should not be above the man's in Japan." The woman shot back, in Japanese of course, that she *should* be on top because she was the better anchor, and smarter too! The two anchors continued to banter back and forth good-naturedly, making the audience howl with laughter. Dee, holding up the offending scrapbook page, and armed only with English, could only flash a smile of surprise mixed with delight.

In Japan, everyone treated Dee with great respect and made the trip great fun. One of our licensors, Uchida of America, owned a ten-story building adjacent to Japan's Disneyland. Uchida made the Blending Blox stamp pads and Dee's brush art markers. As mentioned earlier, Dee had been invited to choose over seventy new colors that doubled the Marvy array. She also named all of them with no suggestions or corrections, an unusual honor for a woman in the Japanese culture.

Dee was sent to introduce American style scrapbooking to Japan. Here she is on the popular television program *Zoom In*. The page shown that she created caused a hilarious stir with the anchors of the show.

Uchida put us up in a hotel that had been a personal favorite of Winston Churchill, and took us to splendid restaurants for Japanese food. They even unsuccessfully tried to find the house in Hayama where Dee lived for one year as a teenager. They included us in a business meeting held in their factory.

Japanese protocol was such that hierarchies were obvious. When we arrived at the Uchida building, we entered an elevator containing the company president who had just arrived at the first floor. We had passed his limousine waiting for him with the engine running at the entrance. He probably was aware of Dee's arrival, but ignored both of us completely. Only after a staff member had showed us all ten floors of the large building were we taken to his office on the top floor where he and his aides were exceedingly gracious and interested in seeing examples of Dee's stamped art.

The next day, the President of Uchida's major competitor invited us to see Tokyo through his eyes. What an unforgettable adventure! We went on a river cruise, ate both lunch and dinner with him, and saw the highlights of the city. He took photos that day and evening and noticed what Dee found interesting in the beautiful stores of the upscale Ginza area. When we returned to our hotel, we found a beautifully wrapped package with lovely papers that Dee had been admiring on top of 8x10 glossy photos retelling the whole day's adventure.

I was originality concerned that he was interested in bringing Dee over to his company, as his products were similar to Uchida's, or that he wanted information about Uchida. He wanted neither. He was just a delightful, generous Japanese man.

Over dinner, I asked him only one question about his company. He wagged his finger back and forth and said, "No business talk, only fun." He never brought up business again during the day and a half that we enjoyed his complete attention. The following year, when he came to attend America's largest craft show, the Craft and Hobby Association Trade show in Anaheim, he took us to one of Orange County's best restaurants. He was gracious to a fault. We saw him each year thereafter and he remained a generous and respected friend.

## LESSON

*Wherever you go, make the most of it.*
*It's how you choose to see the experience.*

# Dee Gruenig's Dream Team Alaska Crafting Cruise

Aboard **Celebrity's Infinity**
on a 7-day exquisite cruise to Alaska

## September 12-19, 2008

from Seattle, WA to Sitka, Juneau and Ketchikan, Alaska

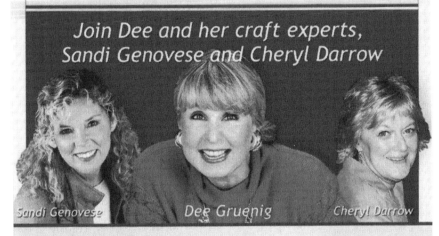

*Join Dee and her craft experts, Sandi Genovese and Cheryl Darrow*

Sandi Genovese     Dee Gruenig     Cheryl Darrow

Learn exciting new ways to stamp, make dimensional cards, an acrylic memory book and much more!

Onboard ship amenities feature timeless elegance, gourmet cuisine and signature service.

Inside Cabin: $1102 pp dbl / Outside Cabin: $1272 pp dbl / Balcony Cabin: $1522 pp dbl

*For more information please call:*
**Drolett Travel**
Hobby and Craft Group Specialists
**800-627-8350**
drolett@drolett-travel.com
www.drolett-travel.com

**X**®
**Celebrity Cruises** ®

Twelve Dee Gruenig cruises permitted bonding through crafting, some led to life long friendships.

# Chapter Twelve

## Invitation to Take People on Cruises

*The great difference between voyages rests not with the ships,
but with the people you meet on them.*

— Amelia E. Barr

Imagine a full week of stamping and scrapbooking on a cruise. The participants on board devoted so much energy and focus to their activities that most of them didn't attend the ship's shows or events. They barely ate dinner! Many stamped and bonded into the early hours of the morning. Many new friendships became permanent.

There were twelve so-called *Dee Gruenig Cruises,* meaning that a designated group among regular passengers travelled together on a ship. Though Dee's name was on the cruise, she did not actually set it up. Wendy and Steve Schwartz, owners of Stampadoodle of Bellingham, Washington sponsored Dee to lead one of the first rubber stamp cruises ever. Naturally this invitation was eagerly accepted!

Cruise participants who sailed with Dee paid for their own cruise, which included instruction. Dee and I were provided complimentary passage by the organizers because the large group purchase made some free cruises possible, and some of the free passage money was applied to reduce fares by a percentage for everyone. The cruise line gave permission to sell supplies to those attending during one of the nights. The cruises maintained their popularity, as there was real value and a great amount of fun available.

Dee usually led seventy-five or more participants who were most excited to stamp and scrapbook. There were always two talented and well-known stamping teachers to join her, making three instructors who had their own following of fans. One such accompanying teacher was the television host of *Do It Yourself*, Sandi Genovese.

Dee's cruises always took place on the huge 3500-passenger Royal Caribbean Voyager class ships because they have large, well-equipped conference rooms serving as oversize classrooms for teaching, storage, and sales. They could easily accommodate a hundred participants with room to spare, and all projects could be left in progress for the full length of the week's cruise.

Most other stamping cruises were held on smaller ships, and instructional classes needed to occur on small tables in a bar or in the dining room, requiring timely setup with immediate takedown and cleanup afterward. There was little privacy in such classes.

All stamping materials were provided for those who attended Dee's cruises. At the end of the cruise, motivated participants could purchase supplies they had been using at greatly reduced prices and often bought new materials as well. Dee and I always had plenty of products on hand and sold most of them so we did not have to ship them home.

The three teachers helped each other and worked hard to make the trip memorable for everyone. Royal Caribbean's Voyager Class had excellent evening shows and I would have to attend them without Dee because even in the evening, she would be still in the classroom, helping her students. She loved the cruises and didn't mind that she missed shipboard activities. She actually preferred to assist the other teachers with their instruction in addition to her own.

The destinations usually alternated between the Eastern and Western Caribbeans. Two of Dee's twelves cruises went to Alaska. Stampers didn't seem to care where they went, and even though there were no classes when in port, some stampers didn't get off the ship for tours, preferring to work on their projects with their new friends.

$\heartsuit$

## LESSON

*Make a place where others can flourish, bond, and enjoy themselves. It comes back to you usually in a form unexpected. If you choose or keep score about the way your gifts should be returned, you will usually be disappointed.*

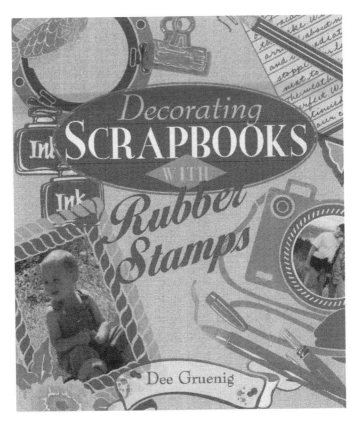

Dee was one of the earliest crafters making scrapbooks. This book, one of ten, sold in both hard and soft cover from Sterling Publishing. It was first to teach the combining of scrapbooking and stamping.

# Chapter Thirteen

## Invitation to Write Best-selling Books

*I want to do something splendid…something heroic or wonderful that won't be forgotten… I think I shall write books…*

— *Little Women,* Louisa May Alcott

*The things I want to know are in books; my best friend is the man who'll get me a book I ain't read.*

— Abraham Lincoln

**D**ee is not a writer. She sees things in color and design, not in the written letter. However, she was invited to write a book and was offered an editor to assist where needed.

Chapelle, Ltd., a publisher that worked with Sterling Publishing Company, Inc. of New York, extended the invitation. Dee agreed almost immediately, though she had never written a book. As with other invitations, she could have declined, but with her continuous expectancy of good things to happen, she willingly went forward.

This resulted in *The Great Rubber Stamp Book.* It had some good examples of stamping, but little instruction about how to get the results of stamp art shown. Also, the presentation of the work and its printing was not what it might have been. Colors that looked good when stamped became bold and brash in the book. I thought her first effort at a book was only satisfactory, but it was the first major book about rubber stamping.

I would have been happy if Dee had sold 500 or 1,000 copies, since at the time rubber stamping was new, unfamiliar, and accounted for only a small segment of the craft industry. I was shocked to find that the book, counting its reprinting, sold an astounding 232,000 copies, of which 160,000 were in hard cover before going to paperback. After the book appeared, stamping began to explode into wide popularity with women over forty. Dee was in the right place at the right time. *The Great Rubber Stamp Book* became the buzz of rubber stampers.

In 1996, the book was featured alone on page one of Sterling's extensive catalog. On that page, it sported a full color photo of the book's cover with a well-written and inviting description from the publisher. Sterling had over 400 titles for crafts in their catalog that year, and a year after the book's release, they sent a letter to book stores that Dee's book had more sales than any of their other titles. Book of the Month Club had picked it up and featured it alone in their own promotions and sales. I received compliments for getting the Book of the Month placement, but knew nothing of the Book of the Month workings. I didn't even know of their interest in the book. Dee and I accepted that unseen hands were guiding the progress of her work.

Chapelle and Sterling both were delighted with the sales. My head was spinning but Dee didn't even blink, as though she expected it.

There's more!

When I made my usual shopping run to our neighborhood Costco store, I came upon a display of stamping kits designed for children. Inside the kit, Dee's *The Great Rubber Stamp Book,* written not for children but for adult stampers, was placed in the center of a clamshell. The book was surrounded by items for children such as a number of rubber stamps, a dozen marking pens, a couple of stamp pads, scissors, paper punches and other assorted objects. The kit's cover, a complex, three-sided, overlapping container with Velcro fasteners, had copied the book's cover on all three sides. If the contents of the kit had been produced in the United States, its cost would have been well over $100. The cost of the kit in Costco was $19.99!

The display was simply a stack of kits sitting on a pallet taller than my six-foot height and about four feet wide. That stack sold out in two days. About a month later, another pallet of the kits sold out as quickly. We have two Costco stores in our area and this happened at the second store as well. I suspected, but am not sure, that it happened at all Costco stores. These books sold at Costco were in *addition* to the 232,000 count that was in Sterling's report. Apparently, Sterling had permitted an Asian firm to make the book the centerpiece of their stamping kit that contained products made inexpensively in China.

Two hardcover books followed that were successful, but did not achieve the sales success of *The Great Rubber Stamp Book.* The second book, *Decorating Scrapbooks with Rubber Stamps,* focused on scrapbooking. The third, *Dee Gruenig's Rubber Stamp Treasury,* emphasized the novel stamping of wrapping paper and envelopes.

Soon, while Dee was sitting in an airport chair, completely asleep, a surprise invitation came from Suzanne McNeill of Design Originals, publisher of how-to craft books. Design Originals was always first to spot trends and to present what was new in crafts. Design Originals published small, focused, thirty-six-page how-to books with everything top quality, including paper and printing. Dee's first book, under license with them, was *Dazzling Designs* and the publisher did a beautiful job. Then, from the same publisher, came *Rubber Stamping With Posh-abilities.* Both did well in sales, especially *Dazzling Designs.*

A competing publisher to Design Originals, Hot Off the Press Publishing, produced two books that were numbers one and two in sales of their five how-to books about rubber stamping. *Stunning Stamping Techniques* was handsomely done, and was the book we were most proud of from this publisher that also published Dee's *Stamp Your Memories with Paper Pizazz.*

Authorship provided Dee a new level of respect and a platform for her to go to another level.

## LESSON

*You don't think you can do something? Get help, be willing to learn, and then do it.*

# Chapter Fourteen

## Invitations to Teach Through Videos and Media

*You are all my guests…*

— Lars Von Trier

aking videos was Dee's specialty, so a "yes" to an invitation to make them was easily forthcoming. In her books, it was a challenge to show and have it understood just how she created art made with rubber stamps. There needed to be additional demonstrations of *how* results were achieved that books could not adequately show. With video and television, Dee could personalize the instruction with enthusiasm and love for what she did. It was if she were right there with the viewer. Users of her rubber stamps encouraged her to make more videos, and she simply loved to teach through them. When you love doing something, whatever it is, you tend to do it better.

In 1988, a company appeared that would conduct home parties to demonstrate and sell rubber stamps. Stampin' Up! extended an invitation to Dee to appear in their early promotional video. The video's purpose was to enlist demonstrators for their home parties.

The two founding sisters appeared in the video for the first fifteen minutes to explain the benefits and expectations of being a demonstrator and sales professional. Next, for twenty-five minutes,

Dee demonstrated rubber stamping, showing how it was done. This was one of the first times Dee had ever appeared on camera.

The three did an effective job with the video. I cannot know for sure, but was told that over a three- or four-year period, several thousand women joined Stampin' Up! to provide home parties. With these demonstrators, SU became so successful that annual stamp conventions were held at the Flamingo Hilton Hotel, right on the Las Vegas Strip.

Dee, working with the founders of Stampin' Up! Lavonne Crosby and Shelli Gardner, to make their video used to hire thousands of associates for their company. It became the largest company in rubber stamping and immensely successful.

Over a period of years, Dee was repeatedly invited to demonstrate stamping at the convention. Once, she was sitting on a raised platform between two giant screens with a talented cameraman filming Dee's hand movements as she worked and explained. At that particular convention, I sat on the floor to take some photos. There were eight hundred Stampin' Up! associates surrounding me, packing a double ballroom.

In that room, I received a glimpse of what it might be like to be a rock star. I had begun to put a few flyers about Dee on chairs, which was not appropriate to do. As I was picking them up, some of the women saw me putting them into the back pocket of my jeans. Then, when stepping on the stage for a brief moment to do some task, the young women rushed the stage and several hands were in my jean's rear pocket, pulling out flyers they thought were being taken away from them. That was my brief ten seconds of Mick Jagger-like fame, an experience a non-singer like me will not forget!

Stampin' Up! became a hugely successful company, the largest single provider of rubber stamps by far. The reason for their success was their pool of talented associates to demonstrate the capabilities of rubber stamps to an excited host in her own home. She would be surrounded by her friends, who would likely catch the stamping fever. And, demonstration establishes proof. Today, with so many independent stores gone due to competition from big box store chains, and online sales, Stampin' Up! remains one of the few engines to promote interest in stamping.

The second experience with making a video was taping one for Rubber Stampede, Dee's second manufacturer of her Posh Impressions brand of rubber stamps. As I remember, it was filmed in a warehouse-like room in Berkeley, California with simple equipment. The result was a bit primitive, and the film was mostly given away for promotions.

One of the first widespread videos to become a big hit was Dee's *The Seven Secrets of Successful Stamping*. The 90-minute video sold in huge numbers. *The Great Rubber Stamp Book* was the first book about rubber stamping to get wide promotion and exposure, and *Seven Secrets* was possibly the first major instructional video to do so. Stampa Barbara produced a good video, but theirs was intended to bring customers into their stores, while Dee's brought customers into any stores and to many venues. The second one, *Twenty Techniques for Sensational Stamping,* sold even better.

The book was needed first, because authorship provides a perception of success. *The Great Rubber Stamp Book* greatly contributed to that perception but took about a year to complete. The Seven Secrets video needed only a few of weeks to prepare and a day to shoot. Dee did a satisfactory job with writing, but was much better before a camera. The lesson for the reader here is to work primarily within strengths, to expand from what comes naturally.

Clearly Dee clearly enjoyed producing art with rubber stamps and creating or endorsing accessories for them. But, beyond that, she wanted to *show* viewers that *they* could enjoy stamping and be successful as well. For Dee, this came through the lens of a camera better than on the pages of a book.

Stamps and clever accessories thought up by Dee and many others turned people into friends during their use because clubs formed so that enthusiasts could stamp together. Friendships were extended further because what was created was usually given away to make others happy. Doing this was a personal transformation for Dee. It was fun for me to be in the presence of what she did. She was simply on fire, with a desire and confidence to share with others. I admit it—I was proud of her.

The two initial videos were followed by eight more, but the first two were especially successful because they were introductions of a new craft activity destined to become popular. It helped Dee's career to be a pioneer in what would become widespread excitement for stamping and scrapbooking with her books, videos, and later, television. She had many new techniques to share in these venues because she was always experimenting.

The final DVD, *Simply Posh,* approached the sales success of the first two. It had the most new material.

We laughed when a woman introduced her four-year-old son, telling us that he had watched one of Dee's videos over fifty times. Dee would say a line or two from the video and the boy would give the next one. The next time we saw the mother, she said her son had to miss two days of school and continued to watch the video while home, making a total of almost a hundred viewings. A better babysitter the mother couldn't find! When the boy sat on Santa's lap that Christmas, he asked for all the correct materials, by specific name, to be able to make some of Dee's projects.

Besides rubber stamping, one of Dee's videos featured instruction in scrapbooking with the sponsorship of Design Originals, publisher of instructional books. Though she was not as well known for scrapbooking as some others, she was one of the first to do and teach it before it became widely popular. As a trailblazer, she loved to make her own scrapbook papers, theme backgrounds, wallpapers, and such. She made photos and art effects large and expansive. She created effects not done before.

An example was a Western album where she put her own riding Levis, bandana and other Western gear on the color copier's glass to create the background for each oversize page that was repeated as the background throughout the album about a favorite ranch. With the color copy machine, she could enlarge the stamp art to *fill* a page or spill over to a double, side-by-side page of an oversize album. She could enlarge still further for posters. This gave a commercial edge for her first store because due to the expense of them, there were few color copiers anywhere. In their initial days, Kinko's copy centers charged two cents for a black and white copy and $3.00 for one in color.

Writers for magazines called Dee's work bold, colorful, original, and imaginative and it was regularly featured in numerous publications.

Crafting Your Career provides further insight into Dee and her friends. The two-hour DVD was produced by Sharlyn and Shannon Harley, founders of T2G Productions, originally with Fox. The DVD is available, with a blog to enjoy as well, at www.InvitationsEverywhere.com

# LESSON

*Improve your weaknesses, but work
and play in your strong suit.*

A highlight of Dee's career was appearing for 10
years on the HGTV's popular *The Carol Duvall Show.*

# Chapter Fifteen

## Invitations to Appear on Television Repeatedly

*"You must do the thing you think you cannot do."*

—Eleanor Roosevelt

As with videos, television was Dee's medium. As far as I can count, she was on television for over ninety segments when all of the appearances on various cable shows were counted. And, as always, the appearances came as invitations.

Her first invitation to appear on television was under the most trying of circumstances. It was 1989, for *The Home Show*, ABC's bread-and-butter show in the morning anchor position. The hour-long show was shot in front of a live audience.

This first experience was an especially tough way for a television debut, because some national emergency was occurring. I can't remember what the emergency was, but it interrupted the programing. The show featured three guests appearing alone in separate segments. Dee was to introduce the new craft of rubber stamping and was originally scheduled to appear for a fourteen-minute share. Just before shooting, interruptions intensified. With the planned preemption of the program shortening her on-camera time to ten minutes, she wasn't sure just how to proceed. She tried to dismiss concern in her thinking but spoke in a low voice.

"I want to go home," Dee whispered to me.

"You have come this far. You *know* you can do this. There can't be any turning back now," I responded.

"You're right," she whispered and immediately became quiet and reflective. Then, Dee stood taller.

During the first commercial break, the director told her that due to additional need for preempting she would have seven minutes on-camera instead of the planned ten. She looked around. The sound stage was immense. The audience, clapping and cheering, was in a separate boxed area at one end of the stage. She had to condense her presentation to the still shorter amount of time and remember that she would *not* be talking to the noisy audience, but talking to the camera.

Dee's very first time on television was ABC's *The Home Show*. Interruptions for news bulletins kept cutting into the program making it a challenge. The show was hosted by Robb Weller, off camera, and Morgan Brittany at right.

In another area of the sound stage, there was a length of tables with four or five soap opera stars and starlets who would be trying rubber stamping for the first time. Both the audience and the tables seemed lost with such a spacious sound stage, and there Dee would be, standing in the middle of the wide expanse before going to the tables to demonstrate stamping. There were at least three large cameras mounted on big rubber tires. They briskly wheeled around the sound stage. When a red light appeared, she was to speak to that particular camera, and *only* that one.

Once again Dee became quiet, shut out the fear, listened

prayerfully, got centered, and was ready to go forward. She was the third and last guest to appear alone. By the time she was actually in position, the director had spoken to her again, telling her she needed to cut her on-camera time once more. With only three minutes available during commercials, she again reorganized in her thinking what she would say and do. She appeared at the end of the program with her featured time reduced to four and a half minutes. But she got through it. She was hooked, and felt that any television exposure after *that* experience should be duck soup!

When *The Home Show* was canceled in 1994, Carol Duvall, one of the *Home Show* regulars, was given her own show on HGTV. Dee was favorably remembered from *The Home Show* and was brought aboard *The Carol Duvall Show*'s second year. She remained for ten years as one of nine guests who appeared often. She was in seventy-two segments. I never heard officially, but *TCDS* was believed to be HGTV's most popular show for most, if not all, of its eleven years.

Again, Dee was in the right place at the right time, with expectancy of good things happening. *The Home Show* and *The Carol Duvall Show* were both invitations to appear. It was almost uncanny. Dee liked to give gratitude beforehand for what she was convinced was God's loving provision, provision available to anyone, including you, the reader.

*TCDS* made Dee blossom, because she was surrounded by the best talent in the craft field. Carol's Christmas shows were extended from 30-minute programs taped daily to hour-long specials shot live every day for one and sometimes two weeks. Dee appeared in every one of them.

Over the years, hundreds of guests appeared on the show. Some who were seen most, such as Dee, displayed distinct personalities that were recognized by regular viewers. They seemed to pick up naturally on what would work, and all of them interacted well with Carol to make the show successful. Dee was the enthusiastic one, eager to show, eager to teach, and then teach some more.

I was told repeatedly how Dee's enthusiasm was contagious and it brought viewers to the show. Her enthusiasm sold a lot of stamps and stamping accessories in stores around the country. Carol and Dee often laughed together, usually right during filming. Once Dee got so excited that Carol took both of her hands and held them down on top of the demonstration table. It got an explosive laugh from the filming crew when after commercials, three minutes later, Carol was still restraining Dee's hands in the same position. As all programs except the Christmas Holiday Specials were taped, the handholding incident could have been edited out, but being hilarious, it was kept in. Laughter from the crew was retained as well. Another time, Dee or Carol dropped a stamp onto the floor. *Both* bent down to pick it up, disappearing from the camera's view so there was no one to see. Though this would normally call for a retake, they kept that in too!

One of the funniest happenings during shooting involved one of the producers, Gary Grossman. It was one of Dee's earliest appearances on the show. I was sitting quietly next to him when he made a spitball as big as a softball and fired it across the sound stage. It flew right between the faces of Carol and Dee as the cameras were rolling! Producer Grossman then sashayed up to Carol, told her she was fired and said, "Dee, take over!"

You never knew just what would happen on the show. On one Christmas episode, the producers brought Dee out of a studio closet, on camera, to a stunned audience. They explained, "We stored her in the closet after the last Christmas show to have her handy for this one."

The other producer, host of ABC's *The Home Show* when Dee appeared for that first scary time, was Robb Weller. With him around, there was always fun when filming. He was a University of Washington cheerleader from 1968-72 who is credited by most for establishing the first football stadium spectator "wave" in 1981 when he returned to lead cheers as an alumnus. During the middle of filming the 2001 Christmas show, the live audience was told that Weller was absent that day, returning to UW to lead cheers at a football game celebrating the twenty-year anniversary of his creation.

During the first day of filming for a new season, there was a compliment for Dee that I will never forget. I was standing quietly when the cameras were ready to shoot. Carol beckoned me to come forward. I quietly approached and she told me to come still closer.

She whispered, "Did you notice that today we have fresh asparagus in the bowl usually filled with potato chips? And did you see shrimp in the other bowl instead of the usual pretzels?"

I didn't remember that the second bowl had shrimp, but had noticed the asparagus in the first. I nodded my head, "Yes."

"Today is the first day of shooting for the new season and I don't want any screw-ups," said Carol. "That's why Dee is my first guest."

Appearance on *Good Morning Arizona*, a morning news and variety program. Dee did some like these between participating at conventions.

I continuously tried to remain in the background and keep Dee out front. I once was foiled, when a woman in a large audience for a Christmas Special had to leave just as cameras were ready to shoot. I reluctantly agreed to be a replacement in her seat. They placed me, as the only man in the audience, sitting directly next to Carol with the camera fixed on the two of us. It is a strange feeling when you feel you should be doing *something* in front of a camera and are doing absolutely nothing.

After *The Home Show*, and before *The Carol Duvall Show*, Dee appeared on various cable and PBS craft shows. Then, after appearances on the CDS, Dee did several *Do It Yourself* television shows with Sandi Genovese as host. Later, Sandi appeared with Dee on her last of twelve Caribbean cruise teaching experiences.

## LESSON

*Shut out fear with prayerful listening. Do not listen to negative or limiting self-talk. Think of what you are doing and not what people might be thinking about you doing it.*

The craft, stationery and gift industries were generous with support of all kinds...all kinds.

# Chapter Sixteen

## Invitations to Lead with Industry Leaders

*Do. Or do not. There is no try.*

— Yoda

hough Dee had no stationery line of her own, she did sell it in our first upscale store and gave a talk about stationery at the New York Stationery Show. Apparently, they liked what they heard because she was invited to be on their industry's Board of Directors. Later, when she had hit her stride with rubber stamping, she was invited to be on the Board of Directors of the Crafts and Hobby Association, the only remaining advisory body for the craft industry. The board contained the heavyweights of the craft industry, including the CEO of Michael's Craft Stores and the CEO of Jo-Ann Stores. Dee was invited to be on the board to replace someone when he couldn't accept the position. As always, her selection was an unplanned surprise.

That is the way things went. For thirty years, invitations kept coming unexpectedly. She continued to accept them and experienced success after she figured out how to perform what was needed.

At the time of the opportunity to serve CHA, Dee was the owner of two stores and known primarily as an artist and teacher. She was not thought of as the president of her little company, and interacting with powerful industry leaders was new for her. On the first day of her work, the Executive Director told her not to say *anything* unless it was important and not to repeat anything someone had said. Because of this, she joked that the first year she said nothing! But, toward the end of her first three-year term, she earned respect when she learned that the CEOs of Michaels and Jo-Ann's had never done much, if any, crafting.

Dee asked both CEOs to sit down and make some things with their own hands so they could see how the products they sold actually worked. This action was respected by the executive director who became Dee's champion, and she was elected for a second three-year term.

The experience of being on the Governing Board was important for Dee's personal growth. It was a treat for me, as well, because I got to accompany her. While Dee was locked up in all-day planning sessions, I was with directors' wives and husbands, enjoying the cities and sights of places we were privileged to visit. The working retreats, lasting several days each, were held twice a year in the most luxurious resorts in the United States and abroad. They were special also because they were something more than we felt comfortable spending such sums of money for.

Occasionally, Dee was asked to speak about business or building a career. An example was Southern California Conference for Women.. That was a thrill for her because some of the other speakers were Oprah, astronaut Sally Ride, and Anwar Sadat's wife Jehan. Anwar Sadat, President of Egypt, had recently been assassinated for meeting Israeli Prime Minister Menachem Begin and President Carter at Camp David to establish a peace agreement between Egypt and Israel. In America and Europe, Mr. Sadat was a hero to most, and a welcome anticipation was certainly in place for Mrs. Sadat. Dee spoke immediately after her, which was exhilarating. Admittedly, the huge room that was packed to hear Mrs. Sadat was not nearly so full for Dee, but what an experience!

# LESSON

*Associate with those most respected and you will become more like them.*
*Strive to be in the presence of those who can teach and inspire you.*

One of only two magazine covers produced by Dee. Color and vibrancy
were often components of her stamped art using her own Posh Impressions.

# Chapter Seventeen

## Invitation to Give Something to Others

*Only a life lived for others is a life worthwhile.*

— Albert Einstein

*A man wrapped up in himself makes a very small bundle.*

— Benjamin Franklin

Dee did many things for others and rarely expected something in return. She didn't keep score, but was generally rewarded in ways unexpected.

In 1988, Dee's first rubber stamps in her infant line of Posh Impressions were presented at the Los Angeles Gift Show. Dee created a colorful display for the area where new products were introduced. The display included six large posters of art made with rubber stamps. One poster featured Dee's Posh Impressions line that she was introducing. Then, she made five other posters featuring stamp art from the five biggest rubber stamp manufacturers. Those manufacturers represented were Rubber Stampede, the company that manufactured our Posh stamps for us; All Night Media; Personal Stamp Exchange (PSX); Hero Arts; and Stampendous. They were all competitors for Dee's new line.

Further, Dee created the posters using the stamp images of each of the other companies and made an effort to stamp in the style of *their* artists. The competing companies that knew of this gesture extended invitations to visit with them in their convention booths. The act of generosity opened the door to lasting friendships with competitors. That was Dee's way.

At conventions, attendees would sometimes follow her around. Dee would stop and talk with them, often inviting them to join her in a manufacturer's booth where she would be demonstrating or teaching. There she would create a card or bookmark for them and sign it with her impressive calligraphy. Dee genuinely liked people and treated them with friendliness and respect.

*The best way to find yourself is to lose yourself in the service of others.*

– Mahatma Gandhi

An invitation came from Meredith Corporation, home of 170 different magazines, including their flagship *Better Homes and Gardens*. The president of Meredith was currently serving as president of the Craft and Hobby Association Advisory Board of Directors (CHA) where Dee was also a member. He wanted to know how rubber stamping worked and so his company asked Dee to fly to Iowa and show them. Dee readily agreed and though her expenses were paid, she asked for no pay for her three days with them.

Four months after Dee's time in Iowa, she received three unexpected visitors. Two editors and a photographer came knocking on the door of our sixth store in Irvine, California. They spent a couple of days interviewing Dee and photographing the store with its creative windows. We thought it would be nice to have a page or two in one of their magazines and were shocked when the magazine appeared. *Better Homes and Gardens Crafts*

*Showcase* had published fourteen consecutive pages of Dee and our final store. It felt a little special when I saw the magazine nestled between *Time*, *People*, and *Redbook* at supermarket checkout lines nearly everywhere I went.

As a result of the publicity, our business boomed, especially when Meredith gave me permission to reproduce those pages in a booklet. It was one thing to say something good about our business, but when *Better Homes and Gardens* did so, especially in a major feature, it packed considerable punch. I printed 7,000 copies of the article in the form of a booklet so that every individual and organization we did business with could see it. The following year, Meredith introduced a new publication, a magazine devoted to scrapbooking. In their first issue, they published ten consecutive pages featuring only Dee's scrapbooks. We had never seen such generous coverage.

Dee's practice was that if you give, and then keep score of what you think is owed you in return, unhappiness can set in quickly because people do not usually pay back precisely as expected or hoped for. Best to give something because it provides you pleasure to do it! That pleasure cannot be taken from you. You *do* get paid back, but seldom in the way or from the person as expected. Working with Dee and the business she founded showed me countless examples of character and the generosity that she expressed.

## LESSON

*Giving to others usually provides more pleasure than receiving.*

Gratitude for protection, situations solved, and overall success was part of the mix and gives one pause.

# Chapter Eighteen

## Invitation to Experience God's Loving Protection

*"Develop an attitude of gratitude, and give thanks for everything that happens to you, knowing that every step forward is a step toward achieving something bigger and better than your current situation."*

— Brian Tracy

*"The way I see it, if you want the rainbow, you gotta put up with the rain."*

— Dolly Parton

At one of our Denver Junior League fund raisers called the Mile High Holiday Mart show, nearly every rubber stamp and supportive product we owned, including the actual booth for the show, were being transported to the show in a U-Haul truck. We had cleaned out almost all of the store's inventory for a trip to participate in three Junior League shows. The inventory was from our first store, nearly all of the merchandise we had, and was valued at six figures. At that time, we were unable to find insurance to cover the month on the road that several shows would require.

A college student had driven to Denver for us the previous

year, so we hired him again. He neglected to tell us that he had become ill during the year and that he hallucinated or passed out when stressed. On the day of his drive, he went to a college class without notifying us. This meant that he had to begin driving eight hours later than scheduled and scramble to make up the lost time, in an old loaded truck, on mountainous roads.

The roads twisted at high altitudes with numerous sheer drop-offs to waiting canyons below. We planned his route carefully a year earlier, but not this time as he had driven well the previous year.

I telephoned Dee, who had flown to Denver a day earlier. "Honey," I said, "has the truck arrived from California?"

"No" she said. "The show will start in twelve hours. I am worried. He should have been here hours ago. Have you heard anything?"

I had heard nothing, not even an expected call about his progress. He was supposed to have arrived two days before the show. No one had seen him.

The young man had told me he was an American Indian and a member of the Church of Jesus Christ of Latter-day Saints church. From our home in California, for seventy-two hours, I called hospitals and Mormon church wards from the West Coast to Colorado. No one had seen him or the truck. No one!

More calls to police, hospitals, churches, and anyone I could think of. I didn't know I could stay wide awake for two full days and nights. I had an impulse to get into my car and drive toward Denver and peer over each cliff into the countless canyons below. Police told me they were looking, but couldn't find the truck or driver. While the stress mounted, Dee felt confident this would be resolved, because we always had evidence of care and protection. We could drive ourselves crazy if we dwelled on the negative.

While I tried to find him from California, Dee was often prayerfully sitting in a stairway, waiting for him to arrive. The show had begun, and she had the only empty booth at the Mile High Holiday Mart. She had nothing else to do but wait to see him. She held to the conviction, as best she could, that a loving

God looked after the driver and after everyone, not only her. This would turn out okay.

Going into the second day of the show, four days since leaving California, with no word of driver or truck, Dee was walking down some stairs. Pam Whitney, a woman Dee knew from her college days arrived at the show and was going up the same stairs. Pam, surprised to see Dee because it had been over twenty years since they had seen each other, asked what was going on.

Now gird yourself for what followed. Dee told Pam what was happening. Pam briefly spoke to two police officers who staffed the show and then went out to her truck where she said she prayed for fifteen minutes. She wanted to drive to a quieter place for more prayer, and as she drove, she headed straight to the truck dripping with parking tickets. It had been left directly behind the state capital building and the police did not find it.

After telling Dee of her find, Pam had the truck towed to the show. Next, she rounded up some people to get the undisturbed contents to Dee's booth where they even helped put everything in place. Next, she towed the truck to U-Haul to exchange it for a truck that had keys. After completion of the show, Pam drove the truck on to the next Junior League fund-raiser.

What an amazing experience! What proof of Divine Love's provision! Pam's good news about finding the truck became everyone's good news at the Mile High Holiday Mart. Dee missed a day and a half of sales during the four-day show, but for our company it was still a success. We were both more grateful than can be expressed.

So where was the driver? Believe it or not, he was in jail. While we bailed him out, the police told us a difficult to believe story. I can't vouch for the accuracy of what we were told, but here it is.

The driver forgot to bring his needed medicine for the long drive. Feeling under pressure to make up the lost time due to his late start, he did make it to Denver but was hallucinating when he arrived. He left the truck where it was found. The driver thought he had left the keys in the truck's ignition and fortunately, that proved incorrect. He had thrown them away somewhere. Miraculously, during those three days, no one had bothered the contents of the truck! Everything was locked and secure, as packed for the trip.

Denver police told us that our driver, not aware of what he was doing, chased a woman who called to a nearby policeman for help. The driver struck the police officer who came to help her. During the struggle, the officer's backup arrived and the driver hit him too. Police carted the driver off to jail.

We paid the driver as he had tried his best and needed the money. I don't think he remembered what he had done anyway. Regarding the stories about what had happened, Dee and I were unsure of what to believe. We only knew what we were told. But locating the lost truck by Pam happened exactly as written, as Dee witnessed the incredible event. As I write this, I telephoned Pam to confirm it happened as I am reporting.

The following year, our driver to that same Denver Junior League show was none other than that amazing, spiritually minded woman, Pam Whitney. She has since become a dear friend. In the summer of 2015, Dee taught a college class about artful creativity and Pam Whitney was her able assistant.

*Every path has its puddle.*

—English proverb

*One loss is good for the soul. Too many losses is not good for the coach.*

—Knute Rockne

Only recently did we discover that we dodged a bullet. About 2005, Dee and I were in her studio working on a promotion when two young ladies knocked on the door. We had most of our Posh Impressions products, licensed by several manufacturers, spread over a large worktable. Each of the products had Dee's signature and photo on the package. There were other products that were not licensed, but had her photo and signature on them as well.

The two women spoke to us briefly while their eyes scanned the table. They seemed strangely delighted about something and left with broad smiles.

The following day, two gentlemen dropped by the studio and introduced themselves as president and vice president of a glove company. They also looked over everything on the table that had been left untouched from the previous afternoon. With so many products containing Dee's likeness and signature, the young ladies and two gentlemen must have thought that there was *no one* in the craft industry as well known as Dee Gruenig. They informed us they were from ProCraft Gloves Company and asked some questions before they left.

The following day they invited me to their headquarters in a nearby city. I found five people, including ProCraft's president and vice president, sitting at a board of directors' table. The president wanted Dee to endorse their Lycra gloves that they believed could be used with comfort for crafting. The gloves were already used in other industries, so they thought crafters would like them as well. Actually, few American crafters wore gloves when they worked, even if what they were doing was messy. They liked to *feel* what they were doing. Other gloves didn't allow them to do this, but ProCraft gloves made of Lycra might make tactile work possible.

Latex gloves were thin, so crafters could feel what they were doing, but they were generally disliked because they made hands perspire. Some believed they were unhealthy, and some people are allergic to latex. Gloves of latex are normally used for a single task and then thrown away.

Lycra seemed a better choice as it was tough and durable. A

Lycra glove was fitted to specific hand sizes and was thin enough to permit tactile feeling while crafting. We were told they could be put into the washer and dryer on a low temperature.

The group in the boardroom put me at the head of the table because they said they didn't know much about the craft industry and they wanted to learn. They wanted someone respected within the industry who could influence Americans to wear gloves when crafting. Clearly, they wanted Dee.

This would prove quite a task because Dee was not as universally known as they had mistakenly believed when they saw the large number of her products and products she endorsed on her studio table.

Before I could ask about payment, I was told that the company expected 300 million dollars in sales and Dee would receive ten percent of the gross. They insisted on putting this in writing. I couldn't believe sales could be anywhere near this much, knowing crafters' preference to feel their work *without* gloves. However, I thought Dee should consider the proposition because ProCraft might be at least somewhat correct.

As compared to other industries, crafting was small, and most craft companies had little capital. Suddenly, ProCraft appeared. Owned by Dominion Resources, a multi-billion dollar member of the Fortune 500, it seemed that great success was possible, especially with financial backing such as Dominion!

Back home, I tried the gloves for strength and longevity by wearing them while using a pick and shovel to enlarge a drain hole in our garden's brick wall. They were truly amazing. After wearing them for hard labor for testing, there was no wear on them at all and crafters only needed them to work with gentle crafting tasks.

Dee and I were driven to their modern factory in Mexico. The factory was large, clean, and the manufacturing process appeared to be state of the art. A machine took a two-inch piece of Lycra and stretched it to twenty inches before it snapped. We were convinced of its apparent durability, and crafting friends liked the "feeling" touch it provided for delicate craft work. Impressed and convinced, we agreed to the proposed license.

Dee's photo and signature were placed on every professionally designed box. Ads and flyers were prepared that had Dee's endorsement prominently displayed. Promotional items were more professionally prepared than any done by our other licensors. ProCraft insisted upon using the best available papers and inks and contracting for full-page magazine ads in crafting magazines. A couple of wholesale distributors were nearly ready to carry the line.

Throughout this promotional preparation, we noticed somehow that Dominion Resources was unhappy with the expenses ProCraft was incurring. My specific task was to get the gloves into the hands of crafters who were known and respected, crafters who had personal followings. If they liked them, they would spread the word. I passed out pairs of gloves to over 100 craft notables. They said they loved them; however, they never *bought* a pair. That should have been a warning!

After a few weeks on the market before major promotion was released, sales of the gloves got little traction. Lycra gloves were considered too expensive at $7.95 a pair when it was possible to buy latex gloves at $18 for a box of one hundred. ProCraft had established a higher price to present a needed profit margin for wholesalers and distributors. The belief had been that crafters would prefer Lycra gloves over latex and that Lycra would last longer for multiple uses, justifying their expense. Both beliefs proved incorrect. Next came a stunner that actually saved our reputation.

Wealthy Dominion Resources owned several small companies that had nothing to do with electric and natural gas power, which is Dominion's domain. ProCraft was one of them. Dominion undoubtedly expected more revenue than glove sales for crafts could possibly deliver, especially so early in their introduction. Therefore, ProCraft was unexpectedly sold to a Japanese company. This made good sense because Japanese often wear both masks and gloves while Americans do not. As far as I know, ProCraft leadership knew nothing about the approaching sale.

Later, we learned more about why the company was sold to a Japanese firm. When ProCraft Lycra gloves had been used for crafts, crafters' hands were surprisingly softer after use. Blemishes disappeared too. Some American crafters wore them when sleeping to improve their skin. I wore them to bed and they made my hands look better as well. Japanese dermatologists discovered that the gloves softened and healed skin, and ProCraft was sold to a group representing them.

There was another problem with the gloves that we did not know about at the time. Though they were extremely durable when newly manufactured, they deteriorated badly, with a short shelf life. We had saved about fifty pairs of gloves for future gifts. A little more than a year later, I tried to put on a pair to wash dishes. They tore easily when I put them on. We tried other pairs with the same results. I knew that humidity, heat, or cold in the garage did not contribute to the deterioration because some pairs were stored in my home office, and they ripped and tore as well.

Fortunately, ProCraft was sold to the Japanese *before* any of the beautifully prepared ads or flyers were released to the public, and before distributors were fully in place. Though some were sold on a small scale and I had given a pair to over a hundred crafters, they were not yet used on a large scale by paying customers. We and our company would have been greatly embarrassed, with damage to our reputation, if a great number of crafters had purchased them.

# LESSON

*Let your loving God take care of you. He knows what to do. If you lose something, or nearly so, don't lose the lesson.*

# Afterword

As mentioned throughout this book, during Dee's thirty-year business career, invitations and opportunities repeatedly appeared for her. Most arrived as a surprise. When we put our own human plans in place, we often didn't get the results expected. Instead, an invitation for something better would appear and we accepted it. This happened consistently for three decades, as long as Dee headed the business.

We both believe in a divine power that created us all and wants the best for us. Thinking this way had the results described in this book. Whatever your faith is, put it to use. Bless others and bless yourself.

Recapping, I had no idea who the woman was who invited me to come in for an interview for a teaching job, resulting in two teaching employment placements with only one interview. We didn't know the interior designer who opened the door for Dee to experience a wider world beyond public school teaching. The invitation to have home parties led to retailing and later wholesaling. Neither of us had heard of the Junior League, but saying yes to participation with them made bigger invitations possible.

The invitations to have stores in two of the leading malls in Southern California were major surprises. The invitation to go on network television and later to appear often on a top-rated cable television show was unplanned. The invitation to write a book with a major publisher that set a sales record, and the invitations to speak at conventions and make lots of videos were unplanned. To land in the licensing lap of possibly the largest craft manufacturer as a licensee, and then nine other manufacturers, were uncontemplated invitations. We didn't ask for any of it. *We could not have humanly planned any of it.* Dee simply had a can-do trust that portals would open to successful ventures. They always did.

Though Dee planned well for everyday activity, she never made long-range plans. So, expect the unexpected, as she did. Expect God's guidance by listening for it with trust. Be grateful for opportunities *beforehand* and then have the courage to act on them. One way to glorify our Maker is to use the talents given us, to be the best we can be at what we do, and to assist others to use their talents too.

## SUGGESTIONS

Choose a belief system that supports and does not hold you back. Monitor your thoughts. Think the best of yourself, of others, and of the world. All around us is negativity in today's world. Lately, edginess, ugliness, and disasters are the trendy things of books and movies. Don't buy into them. Your belief system is important. What you deep-down expect and what you choose to think about most of the time will determine your day, your world, and your success.

So, believe in yourself and believe that your Creator wishes you well. Believe that the Universe is on your side. Also, believe that people are on your side. Why in the world would you want to believe something else? There might be doubters and wet blankets among your friends and family. Love them, but don't buy into their negative thinking, and don't buy into your own. Dare to go forward and don't be concerned about what others think about it. One of Dee's favorite sayings is, "Your opinion of me is none of my business!"

## RETIREMENT

*Don't cry because it's over. Smile because it happened.*

— Dr. Seuss

I will not use the word "retirement" because we are busier than ever with all kinds of good activities, putting to use the experiences learned and shared in this book. I am fortunate to have a mate with a great outlook on life, a loving, genuine best friend, who has grown as she followed her inspiration and accomplished something. I am blessed to know her.

# LESSON

*Listen, let in inspiration, spiritual guidance, and intuition.*
*Then get going.*

This is the way I see Dee and me. I love to
look after her though she rarely needs it.

# Actual Invitations with Dates

None were planned or made possible by Dee's or my own efforts. It would have felt good to take all of the credit. I cannot, and she cannot, because the invitations simply appeared. They, as described throughout the book, arrived mostly from sources unknown or unfamiliar. They came from expectant, trustful listening to God's direction, followed by action taken. Terrific things happened.

Could it be luck? Sure, and it would be like throwing dice and coming up with a winning seven or eleven thirty times in a row. Extremely unlikely.

Following are the major invitations:

**1966:** An invitation from a friend for Dee and me to meet.

**1967:** An invitation for us both to teach United States Steel executives' children in an American school in Venezuela. We worked together and this led to our marriage the following year.

**1972:** An invitation for both of us to teach after only my one interview, in new schools in California upon our return from South America. No applications could be obtained because existing teachers were being pink-slipped statewide. Dee's interview for her position came *after* she was hired.

**1977:** An invitation for Dee to be trained in color, design, and drafting, by a nationally known interior designer, Lee Mink, who designed the top floors and offices of the famous Armand Hammer building on UCLA's campus. Then came an invitation to teach for Ms. Mink.

**1978:** Invitations to design home interiors for friends and acquaintances.

**1979:** An invitation to show accessories used in interior design as a collection for home party gatherings. This began her thirty-year career as president of Posh Presents Inc., doing business as Posh Impressions.

**1980-1998:** Regular invitations to speak at shows and conventions in the United States and abroad on the subjects of gifts, stationery, rubber stamping, and scrapbooking. Among the invitations was the Conference on Women where principal speakers were Oprah Winfrey, astronaut Sally Ride, and others. Dee spoke following Mrs. Anwar Sadat.

**1983:** An invitation to participate in sales for fund-raisers with the Orange County branch of the respected Junior League for nine years, setting two sales records.

**1983-2000:** Features in dozens of magazines about her creativity, art, and retail stores, one example being fourteen consecutive pages in *Better Homes and Gardens Crafts Showcase* magazine followed by ten consecutive pages in their first edition of a scrapbook magazine.

**1984:** An invitation/suggestion to have the first retail gift store that specialized in original and innovative creative work. The store won a national second place award for

Outstanding Achievement In Store Design from *Gifts and Decorative Accessories* magazine, New York.

**1984-1992:** Invitations to participate in sales with additional Junior League fund-raisers all over the United States.

**1988-2005:** Invitations from, and acceptance of, ten manufacturers to incorporate her original hand-done designs and ideas into products that appeared nearly worldwide.

**1989:** Invitation to introduce stamping on ABC Television's *The Home Show*, shot live with an audience.

**1989-1998:** Invitations to teach in competitors' stores.

**1990-2005:** Invitations to appear on numerous instructional cable television shows, including seventy-two segments on the much-watched HGTV's *The Carol Duvall Show* over a ten-year period.

**1991-1998:** Invitation and acceptance to be on the two leading advisory boards of directors for the stationery industry and the craft industry.

**1991-2001:** An invitation to have two temporary holiday stores at prestigious South Coast Plaza Mall, the largest mall in the West and highest in sales in the United States. Success led to a permanent store there, and three more stores elsewhere, for a total of six.

**1992-2005:** Suggestion and assistance to make popular instructional videos to make her instruction available everywhere. There were ten of them.

**1994-1996:** An invitation to teach art instructors in Germany, Korea, Hawaii, Texas, Kansas, and Oklahoma for the United States Army.

**1995-2008:** Invitations to headline twelve rubber stamp instructional cruises.

**1996:** An invitation, with assistance, to write ten books, from three publishers, the first effort becoming the top seller of all books from Sterling Publishing of New York, with nearly a quarter of a million copies sold. Additionally, Dee's work was included in other books written by others.

**1998:** Invitation to be a principal on IdeaForest.com, an online instruction and sales concept that featured nine instructors considered to be the authorities in their fields for nine specific crafts. She was chosen to be the instructor for rubber stamping. This was part of the "dot com bubble" during 1997-2000.

**2001:** Invitation to have a website fan club made for her that quickly had 5,000 rubber stampers choose to sign up as members. This was before MySpace, Facebook, and Twitter were created.

**2003:** Inclusion with Mary Engelbreit and Thomas Kinkade as one of nine "hot names in licensing" published in the principal magazine for the craft trade, *Craftrends*.

**2005:** Invitation to introduce American-style scrapbooking to Japan at the Japan Hobby Show, with 100,000 total attendance and an unexpected television appearance, though other craft personalities were better known for scrapbooking.

# Acknowledgements

Dee Gruenig, who reluctantly permitted me to write this book though she has never actively sought to promote herself, but instead accepted and acted on invitations.

Leonard Szymczak, my writing coach, who encouraged me to write this book and helped me through the rough patches.

Lynn Taylor, talented in-studio creative artist and close companion to Dee.

Our parents who instilled loving and proper values in us.

Rob Bostick and Judi Watanabe of JudiKins for making Posh Impressions rubber stamps available to consumers today.

Vickie Sullivan, Lisa Larsen and Jane Barton who initiated or assisted with excellent original designs for making rubber stamps.

Carol Duvall, for setting an amazing professional example, for laughter, and for camaraderie.

Shelli Gardner and LaVonne Crosby, Founders of Stampin' Up that provided a much-respected platform for progress in the early days of Posh Presents and Posh Impressions.

Cassandra Highly, my personal assistant, who did everything with faithfulness and grace.

Linda Risbrudt, for introducing innovation, beauty and upscale quality into the first creativity store, Posh Presents. Then, saw that it was maintained. Of all of the many talented and special employees over a thirty-year period, Linda remains the one who made it part of her, loved it, and loves its memory today.

Matt Cohen, our faithful webmaster who created Club Posh and then kept it and online sales going.

Cheryl Moore, for being the neighbor who invited Dee to have her first home party gathering in her home that started Dee's three-decade creative career rolling.

Jan Osthus-Kaplan, Program Manager of United States Army Arts and Crafts programs who found Dee and sent her to teach art instructors at military installations at home and abroad.

Yuko Neal, who accompanied Dee to Japan to help introduce American-style scrapbooking.

William Reed, past president of Crafts and Hobby Association (CHA), who encouraged and championed Dee when she was a member of the CHA Board of Directors. He was also the president of Meredith Publishing who invited her to teach rubber stamping to his staff.

Peg Chapleau, loyal bookkeeper, who appeared on the scene after the second store opened and then steadfastly supported the business in ways far beyond counting the beans.

Michael Snellen, CPA, who kept Posh solvent for almost the entire thirty years.

Mike McCooey, President and CEO of Plaid Enterprises; Andrea Grossman, President of Mrs. Grossman's Paper Company; Vince and Ann Dilascia, Owners of Ranger Industries; Go Iida, Chief Operating Officer of Uchida of America; David Wilke, President of Paper Adventures; Kevin Mullvihill, President of ProCraft Gloves; Gary Barbee, co-owner of Sunday International; Sam Katzen, President of Rubber Stampede. These superb manufacturers and others put Dee's designs into products. They were fair, professional, and a pleasure to work with.

Jim and Ricki Bremer, Owners of Tall Mouse, the best example of a complete craft store, who showed professional respect and encouragement to us as competitors and friends.

Managers of stores over a twenty-year period, especially Colleen Hamil, Victoria Bovard, Norma Weiss, and Kimberly Begin, the latter who won the second place National Merchandising and Achievement Award for our first store.

Magazine editors of three craft magazines who supported us in many ways: Roberta Sperling of *RubberStampMadness;* Kelly Herrold of *Scrap & Stamp Arts;* and Cyndi Duncan of *Altered Arts.*

Larry Robinson, a landlord who even made it a pleasure to pay rent, and who should be an example for landlords of the world.

Marilyn Freund, who made us wish we had the opportunity to work with her at All Night Media. She and Bob Bloomberg built an outstanding rubber stamp manufacturing company. Marilyn is not listed as one of our manufacturers because our time with her was so brief due to the sale of her company to Plaid Enterprises. Plaid was a very good thing for Dee.

Wendy and Steve of the Stampadoodle Paper Café, who arranged the first two of what were to become a dozen rubber stamp cruises.

Barry and Gayle Ackerman, who conceptualized, planned, and led stamping retreats for Dee.

Charlene Maguire who to support Dee, championed and led the idea of having an online stamping club called Club Posh before MySpace, Facebook, or Twitter existed.

Deborah Gold, who invited Dee into the Los Angeles Gift Show, giving her broader exposure to a wider world.

Friends Sally Traidman, Grace Taormina, Suze Weinberg, Julia Andrus, and Judy Beard. They showed the way by example and supported with friendship.

Gary Barbee, who made a herculean effort to put Dee's designs into unmounted rubber stamps against formidable challenges.

Haruo Yasoshima, President of Tsukineko of Japan, who taught us what generosity and grace truly are.

Mary Harris who reviewed, edited, and made suggestions for this book.

Fiona Jayde, of Fiona Jayde Media, creator of the book's cover.

Tamara Cribley, of The Deliberate Page, for formatting and overall guidance.

Wendi Liechty of Laguna Beach Media for website creation and design.

Toastmasters International and my local club, Coastmasters, for encouraging me and millions of others to become better speakers, better thinkers, better leaders, and better people.

# About the Author

Charles Warren Gruenig spent thirty-four years as a public school educator, serving as elementary teacher and later a principal. He joined his wife's business halfway through the thirty-year run of Posh Presents, Inc., doing business as Posh Impressions. As Chief Operating Officer of the expanding company, Mr. Gruenig negotiated store leases and contracts with manufacturers. He worked with store managers, catalogs, website, and directed marketing and promotion. None of these tasks would have been needed without Dee whose inspiration, dedication, ideas, and direction drove the company. C.W. lives with Dee near the beach in Southern California. They have been happily married for 48 years.

# Additional Information

To see photos and videos, receive a newsletter, participate in the book's blog, or request a speaking engagement, please visit www.InvitationsEverywhere.com.

You may also share your own personal stories, or tell me how learning of Dee's experiences has been helpful to you.

*Contact warren@PoshImpressons.com*

Made in the USA
San Bernardino, CA
10 August 2015